SYSTEMS LEADERSHIP IN ...EALTH AND SOCIAL CARE

Most leadership development activity in health and social care has been intra-organisational or confined to a particular sector. However, there is increasing recognition of the need to move beyond simple collaboration and partnership and work towards different models of care which involve addressing the whole health and social care system. This is particularly important when addressing complex and 'wicked' problems in a time of resource scarcity.

This book provides a much-needed guide for individuals, professionals, and organisations making the shift towards working in radically different ways in this current climate. It provides a rationale for systems leadership, describing the basic underlying principles behind it and their origins, and explores the various aspects of it, with particular emphasis on the development of systems leaders in health and social care. It also captures good practice, which is illustrated by a number of case studies, and suggests further reading on the topic.

Combining theory with practice, this book will be essential reading for those studying on courses in public service, public policy, health and social care, as well as policymakers and professionals interested in honing best practice.

John Edmonstone is a leadership, management, and organisation development consultant in public services in the UK and internationally with over 25 years' experience in the human resources and organisation development field in the UK NHS, local government and higher education. John is also Honorary Senior Research Fellow at the School of Public Policy & Professional Practice, Keele University, UK.

SYSTEMS LEADERSHIP IN HEALTH AND SOCIAL CARE

John Edmonstone

Routledge
Taylor & Francis Group

LONDON AND NEW YORK

First published 2019
by Routledge
2 Park Square, Milton Park, Abingdon, Oxon OX14 4RN

and by Routledge
52 Vanderbilt Avenue, New York, NY 10017

Routledge is an imprint of the Taylor & Francis Group, an informa business

British Library Cataloguing in Publication Data
A catalogue record for this book is available from the British Library

Library of Congress Cataloging-in-Publication Data
Names: Edmonstone, John, author.
Title: Systems leadership in health and social care / John Edmonstone.
Description: Abingdon, Oxon ; New York, NY : Routledge, [2019] |
Includes bibliographical references and index.
Identifiers: LCCN 2018050056| ISBN 9781138596818 (hbk) |
ISBN 9781138596832 (pbk) | ISBN 9780429487415 (ebk) |
ISBN 9780429945854 (epub) | ISBN 9780429945847 (mobi/kindle) |
ISBN 9780429945861 (adobe pdf)
Subjects: | MESH: Leadership | Delivery of Health
Care--organization & administration | United Kingdom
Classification: LCC RA971.3 | NLM W 84 FA1 | DDC 362.1068--dc23
LC record available at https://lccn.loc.gov/2018050056

ISBN: 978-1-138-59681-8 (hbk)
ISBN: 978-1-138-59683-2 (pbk)
ISBN: 978-0-429-48741-5 (ebk)

Typeset in Bembo
by Taylor & Francis Books

Printed and bound in Great Britain by
TJ International Ltd, Padstow, Cornwall

CONTENTS

ILLUSTRATIONS

Figures

Tables

FOREWORD

As the NHS enters its 'third age', this is a perfect time to reflect on the future of health and social care. What will it take to improve the resilience of our health and social care system? In reality it is a series of systems that function as continually evolving complex ecosystems. Improving the quality of care and doing more with less are no longer sufficient to meet the unprecedented demographic, workforce and funding challenges that health and social care share. The old ways will not deliver the outcomes that matter for our citizens, our workforce and for an affordable and sustainable system. How can we seize opportunities for innovation from integrating health and social care, adopt emerging technologies and draw on the assets and strengths of the community at a time of rapid societal change?

For most of us who strive to disrupt the old ways, the elusive shift towards a new paradigm is at best tentative and generally frustratingly slow. Ambitious system transformation and radical change from which there is no going back are the new end-game for policy-makers, funders, providers, public health organisations and advocacy groups. However, transformation remains elusive despite persuasive evidence on the building blocks and levers for change and how to create the conditions for successful change. This is advice that is remarkably consistent across sectors and cultures and has been around since the advent of John Kotter's (2014) eight-step change model. Evidence matters, policy levers create the right enabling environment, but transformation takes a collective effort from a social movement of people mobilised by committed and courageous leaders.

This book takes a deep dive into leaders, leadership and, in particular, systems leadership as the critical enabler for transformational change. The author presents a conceptual tour de force of the art and craft of systems thinking and systems leadership, from the values, cultures and behaviours that successfully cede power and control, to developing capabilities to inspire and motivate people to take action towards a better, more sustainable future. We learn that this is not a spectator sport.

Relationships matter – building mutual respect, trust and a shared understanding between different professionals, teams and organisations takes time and needs sufficient space for reflection and honest dialogue. This is a long game that needs both tenacity and sustained investment, while holding the line awaiting the anticipated impact. This is impact that defines value that goes beyond productivity and cost-efficiency and looks to create public value and to realise the outcomes that matter for citizens and communities.

These principles of co-creation, collaboration and collective effort resonate with my own experience of introducing new models of integrated health and social care in Scotland. Working with the NHS Scotland Joint Improvement Team for over a decade I wore my 'boundary spanner' badge with pride. Never entirely comfortable with the 'disruptive innovator' label, I am somewhat relieved to discover my new persona as a 'tempered radical'. Good-tempered, I hope!

The author explores the different approaches to systems leadership in health and social care being pursued in the four UK nations. We are offered useful insight into the different context and the 'variable geometry' that influences the rates of progress towards a common outcome. Of course, there is much that we can learn from each other across the four nations, but we must also learn from the experience of integrating health and social care beyond the UK. For this wider insight I would encourage readers to visit the WHO knowledge platform, www.integratedcare4people.org and the website of the International Foundation for Integrated Care – www.integratedcarefoundation.org.

Six short case studies offer personal insights from individuals and teams implementing change across the UK. These vignettes illustrate the power of systems leadership concepts applied to real life situations.

Enjoy the nuggets of wisdom in this book.

Professor Anne Hendry
National Clinical Lead for Integrated Care, Scottish Government
Consultant Geriatrician, NHS Lanarkshire
Honorary Professor, University of the West of Scotland
Honorary Clinical Associate Professor, University of Glasgow
Senior Adviser, Global Health Academy, University of Edinburgh
Senior Associate, International Foundation for Integrated Care

WHO SHOULD READ THIS BOOK?

Health and social care professionals and managers who are studying in order to move towards more senior roles through Masters-level programmes in health and social care and public policy, including MBA courses (although they may find that some of the views expressed in the book are quite challenging!).

Academic staff in higher education seeking a 'primer' in systems leadership in the health and social care field.

Policy-makers and practitioners who are seeking to become, develop or work alongside systems leaders and who are pursuing Continuing Professional Development (CPD) courses or programmes in systems leadership.

The Human Resource Development (HRD) community, especially Organisation Development (OD) and leadership development practitioners in health and social care organisations with lead responsibilities for both commissioning and delivering support to systems leadership; in particular internal and external consultants and change agents who are working in the areas of leadership and system reform.

ACKNOWLEDGEMENTS

Special thanks are due to the following who have helped in the completion of this book:

Charlie Brown, Chief Operating Officer, The Staff College: Leadership in Healthcare

Carolyn May, Senior Development Adviser, NHS Improvement, England

Hugh McPoland, formerly Director of Human Resources, Northern Ireland Health and Social Care Business Services Organisation

Sharon Millar, Principal Lead, Organisational and Leadership Development, NHS Education for Scotland

Julie Rogers, Deputy Chief Executive and Director of Workforce and Organisation Development, Health Education and Improvement, Wales

Diane Taylor, Head, Health & Social Care Leadership Centre, Northern Ireland

Myra Weir, Director of Human Resources & Corporate Affairs, South Eastern Health & Social Care Trust, Northern Ireland

Input to the book was also requested from the NHS Leadership Academy, covering the situation in England. Unfortunately, they were unwilling to contribute and so descriptive material covering the situation in England in Chapter 6 is based solely on material that they have published.

ABBREVIATIONS

ACO	Accountable Care Organisation (England) A single organisation contracted to provide health and social care services to a defined population
ACS	Accountable Care System (England) NHS providers and commissioners and local authorities working together
AI	Appreciative Inquiry
AS	Audit Scotland
CAS	Complex adaptive system
CHP	Community Health Partnership (Scotland). Successor to LHCCs
CLIP	Collaborative Leadership in Practice (Scotland) Leadership development programme
COSLA	Convention of Scottish Local Authorities
CPD	Continuing Professional Development
CQC	Care Quality Commission
FYFW	Five Year Forward View (England)
HEE	Health Education England
HEIW	Health Education and Improvement Wales
HRD	Human Resource Development
HSCB	Health and Social Care Board. Single commissioning body (Northern Ireland)
HSCLC	Health and Social Care Leadership Centre (Northern Ireland)
HSCP	Health and Social Care Partnership (Scotland) Successor to CHPs.
HSSB	Health and Social Service Board: The four commissioning bodies (Northern Ireland) to 2009
IC4IC	International Centre for Integrated Care
ICP	Integrated Care Partnership (Northern Ireland) Proposed network of care providers led by GPs

ICP	Integrated Care Partnership (England) An alliance of local NHS providers working together
ICS	Integrated Care System (England) Revised name for an Accountable Care System
IES	Institute for Employment Studies
IFIC	International Foundation for Integrated Care
IJB	Integration Joint Board (Scotland)
IJIC	International Journal of Integrated Care
ILA	Intensive Learning Academy (Wales)
JIC	Journal of Integrated Care
JIC	Journal of Interprofessional Care
KF	Kings Fund
LCO	Local Care Organisation. Single health and social care provider organisation (Manchester)
LDP	Local Development Partner (England) A regional leadership academy, working in collaboration with the NHS Leadership Academy for England
LGA	Local Government Association (England)
LHB	Local Health Board (Wales) Integrated health care service provider from 2009
LHCC	Local Health Care Co-operative (Scotland) Original voluntary combination of GPs
LSB	Local Service Board (Wales). Public service partnership body between NHS, local government, police and third sector
MBA	Masters in Business Administration
MDT	Multi-Disciplinary Team
MCP	Multi-specialty Community Provider (England). New care model
MHCC	Manchester Health and Care Commissioning. Single health and social care commissioning body (Manchester)
NAO	National Audit Office
NES	NHS Education for Scotland
NHSLA	NHS Leadership Academy (England)
NISCC	Northern Ireland Social Care Council
OD	Organisation Development
OECD	Organisation for Economic Co-operation and Development
PACS	Primary and Acute Care System (England) New care model
PRINCE 2	Projects in controlled Environments. A project management methodology
PSB	Public Service Board (Wales) Public service partnership body between NHS, local government, police and third sector. Successor to LSB
RCGP	Royal College of General Practitioners
ROI	Return On Investment. An evaluation methodology

RPB	Regional Partnership Board (Wales). Statutory body driving strategic regional delivery of social services
RUPT	Rapid, Unpredictable, Paradoxical, Tangled. The environment for all organisations. (See also VUCA)
SCARF	Status, Certainty, Autonomy, Relatedness. Domains of human experience that activate a reward or threat response
SCD	Skills for Care & Development: Sector skills council for people working in early years, children and young people's services, and those working in social work and social care for adults and children in the UK
SCW	Social Care Wales
SfH	Skills for Health. Not-for-profit organisation committed to the development of an improved and sustained healthcare workforce across the UK
SLDF	Systems Leadership Development Framework (England)
SOP	Standard Operating Procedures
SSSC	Scottish Social Services Council
STP	Sustainability and Transformation Plan (later Partnership) (England)
VUCA	Volatility, Uncertainty, Complexity, Ambiguity. The environment for all organisations. (See also RUPT.)
YACL	You As A Collaborative Leader: Leadership development programme (Scotland)

INTRODUCTION

In this book the field of health care is considered as the maintenance or improvement of the physical and mental health of both individuals and communities via the diagnosis, treatment and prevention of disease, illness or injury.

Social care is seen as the provision of social work, personal care, protection or social support services to children or adults in need or at risk, or adults with needs arising from illness, disability, old age or poverty.

Community care is defined as the longer-term care and support for people who are mentally ill, elderly or disabled and which is provided within the community, rather than in hospitals and which enables individuals to live in both independence and dignity and to avoid social exclusion or isolation. This description is an elastic one and can be taken to include, for example, some of the activities of hospices, prisons, the probation service, the police and clergy, as well as the independent, charitable and voluntary sectors, sometimes known as the 'third sector'.

Integrated care is care that is person-centred, coordinated and tailored to meet the needs and preferences of an individual, their carer and their family. It means moving away from episodic care to a more holistic approach to health, care and support needs, that puts the needs and experiences of people at the centre of how services are organised and delivered. Integrated care is often place-based. Place-based care involves local service providers collaborating and sharing the resources available to them to improve health and care for the populations they serve. The concept extends also to the planning and commissioning of such services (Health and Social Care Committee, 2018).

Likewise, in this book leadership is seen as a 'social influence process, through which emergent coordination (making social order) and change (new values, attitudes and behaviours) are constructed and produced' (Bolden, 2004). It is essentially therefore about the making and mending of working relationships between people and organisations in order to get things done.

While some of the health and social care services are delivered by 'statutory' agencies (particularly by the National Health Service and by local authorities), others are delivered by both the private sector and by the third sector, i.e. not-for-profit, social enterprise, charitable and voluntary and non-governmental organisations. In practice the boundaries between these different organisational, professional and geographical areas have been, and continue to be, blurred and the need for greater collaboration, partnership working and even, in some instances, organisational merger, particularly between statutory agencies, has been increasingly emphasised over many years.

Whatever the nature of these organisations, one major difference between the bulk of them and most industrial, commercial and financial organisations located in the private sector is that in the latter case there is what has been termed the 'reconciling function' of profit (Hampden-Turner, 1992). In the services which are the focus of this book there is typically, for most, no such reconciler, especially since they are always part of a much wider system. The purpose of these organisations is therefore not primarily to make money (although some may aim to do so) but instead to make a practical difference in terms of social change and improvement.

Both sides of the health and social care system (but perhaps especially the NHS) tend to have a self-referential habit of mind exemplified by a 'not invented here' attitude and subsequently view the 'system' as either health care only or social care only; that it is 'our system' rather than 'the system', and so inevitably the perception to date has largely been one of self-talk within each sector. For example, the need to pay attention to the electoral cycle and to build political support for change through local authority councillors is something which historically has largely been countercultural to the NHS. Moreover, there may be a tendency (again particularly in the NHS) to over-intellectualise and to over-complicate the understanding of systems leadership with little impact on the day-to-day experience of service users, the professional staff who work with and for them and the communities in which they are based.

Local government may well even possess greater expertise with regard to systems leadership than the NHS, not least because, since at least the mid-2000s, many local authorities have increasingly come to see their role as leading across boundaries and being an enabler, bringing together groups of people who affect what happens in their area; becoming 'place shapers' or 'anchor institutions' in their community, rather than just service providers. This is in major contrast to the NHS which is clearly largely perceived in the wider society as being solely a service provider

It is quite obvious that we are only in the 'foothills' with regard to the development of systems leadership in health and social care and that it is very much an emergent activity. It should not be underestimated how challenging is the integration of health and social care, but local health and social care systems will increasingly be propelled towards more collaborative, diverse, inclusive and outcome-focused approaches, whilst seeking to maintain quality, compassion, financial balance and effective individual performance. It therefore implies such organisations working together to mobilise assets in the local community and collective capabilities in order to improve the quality of health and social care for individuals and local populations, while ensuring the wise stewardship of taxpayers' money.

Given the self-referential habit of mind mentioned above, it is also noticeable that much of the rapidly-growing literature on systems leadership emerges from, and is therefore orientated either largely towards, the NHS only or local government only. This book aims to remedy that situation by drawing upon emerging good practice in both areas and by introducing, and hopefully demystifying, a topic that is increasingly relevant in public services, but is not always either well-understood or applied.

Regarding health and social care as a local system places demands upon local leadership that far exceed any organisational leader's reach of conventional power, control or even understanding. Whilst this book seeks to draw together these different strands it can therefore inevitably only be one person's snapshot at one particular point in time.

Chapter 1 of the book sets the context of change and complexity as the 'new normal' for all organisations where the conventional response is to increase competence. Instead, it is proposed that the emphasis should be on capacity. The chapter identifies three kinds of problems which organisations face and notes that 'wicked' problems are frequently located in health and social care, and that leadership is required to address them. While viewing organisations as machines has been the norm, it is suggested that seeing them as complex adaptive systems offers a better 'fit'. The nature of health and social care organisations is examined, together with approaches to their development, before concluding that systems leadership is the preferred way forward.

Chapter 2 asks the questions 'Who are systems leaders?' and 'What do they do?' before describing an authorising environment for systems leadership. Six 'ways' of systems leadership are identified and the factors that facilitate it are specified.

Chapter 3 considers what kind of people we are looking for (and at) in systems leadership, before delineating the important difference between leader development and leadership development. The field of adult learning is explored, with special emphasis on the ladder of inference, single- and double-loop learning and reflection. Mind-sets that limit thinking on leadership are identified, together with their antidotes, before an alternative approach is described, which outlines what is needed in order to learn systems leadership. Principles for designing learning and development for systems leadership, including learning 'architecture' and 'ingredients' are offered.

Chapter 4 indicates what is wrong with current approaches to change management in health and social care and suggests an alternative for systems leaders, before emphasising the importance of sustainability, spread and application. The importance of considering the anxiety raised by change is also addressed.

Chapter 5 examines the challenges of evaluating systems leadership.

Chapter 6 considers the four very different approaches to integrated care and systems leadership adopted in the four parts of the UK.

Chapter 7 offers alternating vignettes and personal accounts from places and people involved in systems leadership.

Chapter 8 attempts to draw out the lessons learned about integrated health and social care and systems leadership across the four parts of the UK.

Chapter 9 briefly offers some final thoughts on the nature of systems.

Finally, possible further ways of addressing the issues covered in the book are offered; additional reading on the topic is suggested and the meanings of the main acronyms are provided.

References

Bolden, R. (2004) *What Is Leadership? Leadership South West Research Report 1*, Centre for Leadership Studies, Exeter: University of Exeter

Hampden-Turner, C. (1992) Foreword, in Common, R., Flynn, N. and Mellon, E., eds, *Managing Public Services: Competition and Decentralisation*, Oxford: Butterworth-Heinemann, viii–x

Health and Social Care Committee (2018) *Integrated Care: Organisations, Partnerships and Systems*, London: House of Commons

Kotter, J. (2014) *Accelerate: Building Strategic Ability for a Fast-Changing World*, Boston: Harvard Business School Publishing

1

WHAT DO WE MEAN BY SYSTEMS LEADERSHIP IN HEALTH AND SOCIAL CARE AND WHY IS IT NEEDED?

This chapter will explore the world in which health and social care organisations find themselves – where change and complexity are the 'new normal' and where volatility, uncertainty, complexity and ambiguity are the backcloth. It will examine the notions of competence and capability as means of addressing this world and will consider the different kinds of problems which such organisations face. Seeing local health and social care as a complex adaptive system is offered as a useful way of working in the face of such a challenging environment, given the particular nature of such organisations. The development of these organisations and the people within them calls for going beyond collaboration towards co-evolution and systems leadership is posited as the way ahead.

Change and complexity as the 'new normal'

Anyone faced with the challenges of working in, and leading and managing, all organisations, but particularly health and social care organisations, in the early 21st century faces a whole series of challenges. These include:

- Working in the continuing aftermath of the 2008 global financial crisis, with the austerity and employment uncertainty which that entails. It means working in an extremely harsh resource climate where both financial and political demands focus attention largely on short-term targets, yet the need for more creative and longer-term thinking is probably greater than ever, while short-term pressures and expectations actually generate and encourage pre-existing 'silo' working within and across health and social care.
- High and growing levels of public expectation of what health and social care services could and should deliver to local and national populations, in terms of quality, choice and accessibility. In this respect, the public has become

increasingly less tolerant of the range, quality and accessibility of current provision and more demanding of future provision. There is therefore an urgent requirement to balance the short-term operational delivery of health and social care services with longer-term and more strategic innovation in those services. Yet there is little or no time or space available for the much-needed long-term joint horizon-scanning activity which could identify exactly what is and is not possible in terms of service delivery.

- Significant social and cultural change, including the growth of multicultural communities in some parts of the UK, and changing (and contested) attitudes towards such issues as obesity, alcohol and drug abuse, abortion and towards welfare provision (previously called 'social security') generally.
- Changing demographics, with an increasingly aging population (often exhibiting long-term conditions and combinations of long-term conditions) and a major shrinking of the younger workforce recruitment pool from which health and social care professionals and other staff have historically been drawn. Frozen or capped salaries available for front-line staff and resultant staff shortages make recruitment and retention (for example in domiciliary care) much more difficult, and taken together with negative media coverage, consistently generate a public 'crisis' image.
- An increase in the numbers of dual earner couples and of workers with family care-giving responsibilities. Despite this, an increase in reported loneliness, especially in the case of both the elderly and the young, but not confined only to those age groups. Loneliness can be about feeling alone even when surrounded by other people and is about the quality of connections with others, rather than the number of social relationships. It is something of a paradox that in a modern, densely populated urban society, there is a shortage of friendship and good relationships, because although people are together, they are also separate (Wilkinson & Pickett, 2018). A danger is that, as a consequence of austerity, the reduction or closure of local services providing such a sense of community and providing vital support may further enhance such loneliness.
- For those in full-time work, the UK has some of the longest working hours in Europe. There is also an unusually high percentage of part-time workers for whom average working hours may be short but many of whom appear to want full-time work but simply cannot access it. This relates to the growth of the 'gig economy' of self-employed people on short-term or zero-hours contracts, with around 25% of the UK employed population being identified as part of this 'precariat' (Standing, 2011). This 'insecure cohort' is less-qualified, has limited job autonomy and significantly less financial security (Williams et al., 2017). They are potentially vulnerable to fluctuations in working time and therefore pay levels, short notice of working schedules and experience a degree of precariousness in terms of a lack of employment rights (Broughton et al., 2018).
- Social mobility has become so frozen that apparently it would take five generations for poorer families in the UK to reach the average income, while higher

earners get bigger rewards and consolidate wealth for the next generation (OECD, 2018). Such growing inequality in UK society produces powerful psychological effects. When the gap between rich and poor increases, so does the tendency to self-define and define others in terms of superiority and inferiority. Low social status is typically associated with elevated levels of stress and rates of anxiety and depression are intimately related to the inequality that increasingly makes that status paramount (Wilkinson & Pickett, 2018).

- A decline in a previous culture of deference to both authority and expertise, largely fuelled by an explosion in the availability and usability of information, much of it digitally-based. A corresponding collapse of confidence and trust in any kind of traditional authority, but especially with those institutions and individuals with claims to expertise (Peston, 2017).
- A growing emphasis on diversity and equality at work and in society as a whole and a growing intolerance of sexism, racism and misogyny. Alongside this, evidence of a growing intolerance of minorities and of increased polarisation within society verging, at times, on xenophobia. This can be amplified by what some observers consider a 'toxic' media, especially via certain newspapers and social media.
- Powerful drives to increase efficiency and to improve quality simultaneously – to do 'more for less'.
- Continuing intra-organisational restructuring or reconfiguration, often known as 're-disorganisation' and typically involving de-layering, down-sizing and the merging of roles or of whole organisations, often resulting in job losses, enhanced uncertainty and a sense of heightened anxiety for the staff concerned (Ballatt & Campling, 2011).
- Uncertainty with regard to the future associated with Brexit – the UK's departure from the European Union. This includes the reluctance of people from the EU to consider full or part-time employment in the UK, especially important where historically health and social care services have been reliant upon them. The potential ending of free movement has a major impact on the adult social care workforce. Seventeen percent (222,000) of social care staff in England are foreign nationals and in 2018 there were 90,000 unfilled social care vacancies, a vacancy rate of 6.6%, compared to an average of 2.5% across the economy (Global Future, 2018).
- As a consequence, increased experience of complexity and ambiguity both within and between health and social care organisations.

All this produces a sense of being caught in a 'perfect storm' of increasing public need, demand and expectation, coupled with a decreasing resource and staffing capacity. As a result, health and social care organisations seem to be on a journey from an old to a new world, as Table 1.1 reveals. This, in turn, means that the work roles that people enact are also shifting, as shown in Table 1.2.

TABLE 1.1 Moving from an old to a new order

Old world	New world
Low complexity, slow change	High complexity, fast change
Learning has a long shelf-life	Learning has a short shelf-life
Senior people know best	Knowledge is scattered
Someone, somewhere, knows	No individual can pretend to know
Doing more of the same is the rule	Innovation is the rule

TABLE 1.2 Shifting roles

From 'I manage'	To 'I lead'
My team reports to me	I am part of a virtual network
I have a hierarchical role	Influencing is the way forward
I understand what is happening	I can only have a partial understanding of what is happening
I have fixed objectives	I take the lead on issues
What I have to do is clear	I cope with ambiguity
I manage by fixing things myself	I lead teams to deal with things
I manage from my knowledge and experience	I lead without knowledge and experience

A VUCA/RUPT world

The characteristics described obviously do not apply only to health and social care organisations, but are manifest in some form or other across both public, private and third sectors on both a national and international basis. They are summarised by the notion of 'VUCA', which stands for:

Volatility: The type, speed, volume and scale of economic, social and organisational change forces and catalyses events to an extent never experienced before.

Uncertainty: There is a lack of predictability with regard to the future and a much greater likelihood of surprises occurring without everyone having an enhanced awareness and understanding of both issues and events.

Complexity: There are multiple forces and factors in play and, as a result, issues become confounded, with no simple cause-and-effect sequence to events and activities being observable.

Ambiguity: There is a lack of precision and there are multiple meanings of the same event possible. Reality can appear 'hazy' with a greater potential for misreading and misunderstanding exactly what is going on.

Social pressures and trends, heightening expectations, the power of social media, globalism on the one hand and localism on the other, together with the continued existence of social, health, housing and policing issues all affect people and their communities – and all contribute to volatility, uncertainty, complexity and ambiguity.

The leadership implications of these characteristics are:

Volatility: Leaders face challenges that, while not necessarily hard to understand, may be unstable, unexpected or last for an unknown length of time.

Uncertainty: Leaders face challenges where the original cause may possibly be known, but a lack of supplementary information serves to shroud the process of change management and the effects can appear diffuse.

Complexity: Leaders face challenges in dealing with a multitude of interdependent and interacting variables across and beyond the boundaries of their organisations.

Ambiguity: Leaders face the challenges of 'unknown unknowns' where there are unclear relationships between cause and effect.

An alternative concept is that of a 'RUPT' world, which is rapid, unpredictable, paradoxical and tangled:

Rapid: Leaders face overlapping challenges, in multiple domains, which occur and re-occur and need to be overcome at pace.

Unpredictable: Leaders face unexpected challenges which, despite thorough and well thought-out strategies and governance, can rapidly challenge underlying assumptions and cause a reframing of thinking.

Paradoxical: Leaders face challenges in polarity. Rather than providing one solution (either this *or* that), challenges need to be embraced as polarities (both this *and* that) to be addressed in both the short and long term.

Tangled: Leaders face interdependent challenges across and beyond the boundaries of their system.

Within this often chaotic environment, rapid and unpredictable paradoxes are embedded in tangled multi-causal relationships. In order to work effectively in such contexts, leaders need to develop (both within themselves and also across the system) a learning capability (see below) where the majority of learning occurs in association with real-life challenges (Till, Dutta & McKimm, 2016). This is addressed in detail in Chapter 3.

Competence and capability

The most popular means which has been adopted to deal with this omnipresent VUCA/RUPT reality has been an emphasis on increasing the competence of key people (i.e. those who are called leaders) in work organisations – and hence to the recent popularity of competency-based approaches to education and training.

Competence is concerned with what individuals know or are able to do, in terms of their knowledge, skills and attitudes, as expressed in their observable behaviour. Much work has been undertaken to analyse, define and publicise what organisations, functions, professions or whole sectors of society deem as desirable competences. Competence obviously works well with 'tame' issues (see below) where the challenges concerned are both clear and unambiguous and where tried and tested solutions can be applied. It suffices when there are high degrees of certainty and agreement and where the tasks to be done and the contexts or settings in which they are to be accomplished are both familiar. It also reflects an 'instrumentalist' and reductive view of learning where, for every predetermined role, there are agreed competences that need to be defined and then achieved. In reality, however, there can be no single set of competences that can capture everything that leaders do, because leadership is as much a collective as an individual activity, is surrounded by complex emotions and politics and is context-specific. It is therefore contentious to claim that there could be a single generic competency-based model of desirable behaviour to work in such complex contexts. It may be, therefore, that the very act of prescribing a set of competences (as outlined above) actually limits the potential emergence of capability (see below).

The picture painted above is certainly not an accurate description of a VUCA/RUPT world and increasingly both individuals and organisations find themselves in situations where there is little certainty and agreement; where both tasks and settings are unfamiliar and where the old and familiar solutions simply do not work. What is required here instead is a form of learning agility called *capability*, which is effectively a form of future-orientated potential and which is concerned with the extent to which individual employees as learners can cope with uncertainty, can adapt to changing situations, can generate new knowledge and can continue to improve their performance (Edmonstone, 2011). It involves a psychological flexibility or 'mind-set', which can react and change swiftly and energetically in response to changing circumstances. It implies continuous renewal and reinvention – learning, unlearning and relearning. For people working in health and social care such capability entails (Eraut, 1994):

- A primary concern for, and an understanding of, service users and their carers.
- An ability to read and analyse a particular situation and to respond creatively to what is seen.
- The ability to draw upon a number of different approaches and to discriminate between them, based upon the merits of each – a personal repertoire.
- A willingness to continuously learn by experiment, reflection and review of experience.
- A concern to work by trial and error – but systematically.
- The ability to theorise about practice during practice – to turn instinct into insight by thinking about what one is doing as one works and arguing about it in one's head and with others.
- From this, the ability to draw out the theory underlying actions.

- The ability to relate personal theory and practice to wider considerations of theory and practice – to self-evaluate practice in order to improve it.
- A concern with knowledge in use and the creation of future knowledge.
- An understanding of, and a concern with, the role of the profession in society.

Increasingly people and organisations have to cope on a regular basis with complex and uncertain situations where all the previously operated knowledge and both the related and preferred routines fall short of, or simply do not fit with, what is happening. In such cases, what works is clearly not a simple adherence to the previously known and trusted procedures, a pretence that surprise elements just do not exist or an expansion of the current practices in order to 'nail down' the problem. Instead it implies attention to effective working relationships and to the specifics of the particular setting or context within which people work. Learning needs to reflect the lived reality where action transpires and where people can be found engaging with their colleagues on real problems. This is shown in Figure 1.1.

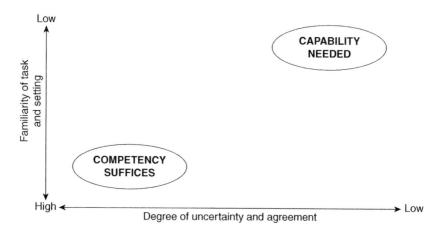

FIGURE 1.1 Competence and capability

As a result, it is important to recognise that in working in a VUCA/RUPT world the defined technical and explicit knowledge that is associated with competence is simply not enough and that the development of that learning agility called capability involves also valuing practical and tacit knowledge. Explicit knowledge, for example, is appropriate for 'technical' challenges, while tacit knowledge is more relevant for 'adaptive' challenges, which involve negotiating a way through ambiguity with other people (Heifetz, Grashow & Linsky, 2009), a point which is further pursued below. This is shown in Table 1.3.

TABLE 1.3 Technical (explicit) and practical (tacit) knowledge

Technical (explicit) knowledge	Practical (tacit) knowledge
Typically codified and written in policies and rules	Typically expressed in practice and learned only through experience
Based on established practice	Based on established practice modified by idiosyncratic understanding and technique
In accordance with prescription	Loosely, variably, uniquely. In a discretionary way based on personal insight
Used in clearly-defined circumstances	Used in both expected and unexpected circumstances
To achieve an envisaged and familiar result	To achieve an indefinite of novel result
Emphasis on routine – method, analysis, planning	Emphasis on non-routine – variety, invention, responsiveness
Focus on well-defined problems	Focus on poorly-defined problems
Generalisable	Locally relevant

Three kinds of problem

Keith Grint (2008) has identified three kinds of problems which all organisations (including health and social care organisations) face. They are:

Critical problems: This is where it is obvious that a short-term and self-evident crisis exists, often at an immediate tactical and operational level. There is virtually no uncertainty at all about what needs to be done; there is little or no time for discussion, debate or dissent and even coercion may be deemed to be ultimately permissible if the outcome is seen as being for the public good. This is the arena of the *Commander* and the message here is: 'Just do what I say, it really doesn't matter what you think.'

Tame problems: This is the area of 'puzzles' which just like crossword or jigsaw puzzles ultimately do have a solution. Tame problems:

- Can be described by a fairly clear and simple statement and where the root causes of the problem are either already known or are relatively easily discoverable.
- Exist where the degree of uncertainty which is associated with the problem is limited and where the situation is stable, predictable and unambiguous. Such problems are therefore constant and do not fundamentally change over the passage of time.
- Have broad agreement between all the interested parties about what 'success' would look like.
- Respond positively to the well-known tools of rational planning and management. In particular, they are largely amenable to project management approaches.

- Are often subject to an organisation's Standard Operating Procedures (SOPs).
- Are marked by the fact that previous experience and practice with the same or similar problems are useful guides towards a solution. So the 'recipe' contained in the 'cookbook' is essential and assures replicability for further efforts, so that the same outcome results are guaranteed every time.
- Have definitive and optimal solutions which would apply in any setting or context – and are therefore transferable.
- Have a clear 'stopping-point' so that it is clearly understood when a solution has finally been reached.
- Can easily be objectively evaluated.

Tame in this context does not necessarily mean simple because a tame problem may be complicated technically. Tame problems are also largely operational problems mainly concerned with organisational efficiency and with looking 'inwards and downwards' and focusing on issues of control and performance. They are usually immediate and short-term and emphasise the maintenance of consistency and the need for correction of deviations from required targets or standards. They are thus the subject of what is known as single-loop learning (see Chapter 3).

With tame problems it is the role of the *Manager* to engage the appropriate process to solve the problem and the message is: 'I've seen this problem before and I know what process to apply in order to solve it.'

Wicked problems: The notion of 'wicked' problems originally emerged in the 1970s in the United States in the context of social and urban planning. It became clear that problems of social policy could not be described definitively and in a pluralistic society there was often no undisputable public good and no objective definition of equity. Such policies cannot be meaningfully correct or false and so there are no 'solutions' in the sense of definitive or objective answers (Rittell & Webber, 1973), but they *can* be progressed. Sometimes described as 'Saying yes to the mess' (Stacey, 2002), wicked problems have none of the clarity of a tame problem. Instead they:

- Are problems with no definitive formulation that provides all the information needed in order to describe it, to break it into manageable chunks and to solve it.
- Are characterised by a high degree of uncertainty.
- May appear to be novel and never to have been encountered before.
- Are usually longer-term and more strategic in nature.
- Interact with, or are 'nested' within, other problems and cannot simply be addressed in isolation, so it is difficult to separate the parts from the whole.
- Will appear 'fuzzy', that is, unclear, incomplete, possibly contradictory and often paradoxical.
- Sit outside single professional and managerial hierarchies and exist across multiple organisational boundaries.
- Represent uncharted territory, where there is no fixed template or agreed way of doing things.

- Defy rational analysis and planning because logic-based linear approaches to problem-solving simply do not work with such highly complex systems with multiple players and often conflicting pressures and motivations.
- While expertise can help, on its own it is simply not sufficient and effective working relationships are therefore key.
- May appear to 'shape-shift' as they are worked on.
- Have multiple perspectives on what exactly the problem is and what the right way forward might possibly be.
- Are strongly related to the particular context or setting in which they exist.
- Previous experience and practice appear to be of little help towards any resolution.
- Progress to be made will require both individuals and organisations to change their mind-sets and behaviour, to learn new ways of working and to choose between contradictory values.
- What exactly 'success' in addressing the problem might be is difficult to define.
- Have no 'stopping rule'. It is impossible to say that a wicked problem has been solved, just that time, money or patience may have run out.
- Solutions to wicked problems are not true-or-false, but good-or-bad. Evaluation cannot ever be objective and always requires judgement.
- Resolution of the problem may even, in turn, create further problematic issues.

Wicked problems are hard to describe and so defy the 'rational' analysis which is associated with tame problems, not least because, due to multiple complex inter-dependencies, actions taken towards resolution often tend to lead towards unintended consequences. As a result, they are seldom completely 'solved' but lead into other related problems. They often require joint working between different organisations, all of which have a different stake in the problem. Logic-based and linear approaches to problem-solving are not an effective approach to such wicked problems which are typically characterised by paradox. The biggest danger is to act on the basis of thinking that we know what to do in such cases, rather than to start from being open about not knowing, and proceeding by questioning and inquiry.

The alternative is to undertake what has been called 'bricolage' – a stitching together of a diverse range of actions and initiatives using whatever resources are at hand. Bricolage involves processes of improvisation, experimentation and exploration. The term derives from the French verb '*bricoler*', which means to fiddle about or to tinker – the ability to make do and use whatever is to hand or to make the most of what we have. Being a 'bricoleur' involves inventiveness – an ability to improvise a way forward without obvious tools or help by imagining the possibilities.

One school of thought (Sarason, 1978) also holds that health and social care issues are quite distinct from physical/mechanical problems and are therefore not actually capable of being worked on by the rational-empirical scientific method of problem-definition and solution. Such issues may be intractable – that is, not permanently solvable – and such intractability may mean accepting the imperfectability of human beings and of society, deeply-rooted in the human condition. No once-and-for-all solution is possible. Instead, such problems have to be addressed over and over again depending upon the idiosyncratic context (time, place and historical circumstances). So any 'solution' can therefore only last until the problem recurs in another form, as the problem can never be eliminated or ignored. Such problems may therefore be the inevitable consequences of human diversity and the social structures associated with it.

This is the arena of the *Leader* who has to engage in collaborative dialogue with all stakeholders and to craft a partial, emergent or 'clumsy' solution, that is, a 'good enough for now' decision that takes the issue on a stage. The message is: 'I've never seen this problem before and we need to get a shared view on what to do about this.'

Others have previously identified the existence of wicked problems, without describing them as such. For example, as long ago as 1969, Laurence Peter asserted that: 'Some problems are so complex that you have to be highly intelligent and well-informed just to be undecided about them' (Peter & Hull, 1969).

Alfred Sloan, the founder of General Motors, is famous for Sloan's Dilemma, which can be phrased as:

> 'Gentlemen, I take it that we are all in complete agreement on the decision here?'
> Consensus of nodding heads.
> 'Then I propose we postpone further discussion of this matter until our next meeting to give ourselves time to develop disagreement and perhaps gain some understanding of what the decision is all about.'

And the American journalist H. L. Mencken (1982) is famed for saying: 'For every complex problem there is an answer that is clear, simple and wrong.'

More recently it has been proposed that:

> It is time that we stopped and stood back and looked at leadership not as a series of problems that can be solved, but as a series of contradictory, puzzling and obscure concepts that need to be managed and lived with.
>
> *(Bolden, Witzel & Linacre, 2016)*

These warnings are important because there appears to be a strong tendency within most health and social care organisations to either assume that all problems are actually tame in nature or to pretend that what are wicked problems are in fact tame, and therefore amenable to being worked on only by rational analysis and planning. In fact, what may seem like the easy way out by applying such approaches usually leads straight back in. Such familiar solutions can not only be ineffective, but can also be addictive and hence dangerous. It has been suggested that: 'Our learnt instinct is to troubleshoot and to fix things – in essence to break down the ambiguity, to resolve any paradox, to achieve more certainty and agreement and to move into the simple system zone' (Plsek & Greenhalgh, 2001).

From a slightly different perspective Ronald Heifetz has identified tame problems as 'technical challenges' and wicked problems as 'adaptive challenges' (Heifetz, Grashow & Linsky, 2009).

The challenges which health and social care organisations face are increasingly wicked problems and, of course, the integration of health and social care is itself a wicked problem, requiring different approaches to be devised. A useful way forward is to consider the field of health and social care as a complex adaptive system.

Complex adaptive systems

The ways in which we have typically viewed all organisations have been through the use of metaphors (Morgan, 1986) – that they are 'like' something else. For many years the most-used metaphor for work organisations has been that of the machine, where the emphasis is on predetermined goals and objectives and where the organisation is expected to work in a systematic, efficient and predictable manner. For over 150 years economic theory has reinforced such biases towards mechanistic models and metaphors (Raworth, 2017). This can, of course, sometimes result in a lack of adaptability and a dehumanising experience for those working within such frameworks. This machine metaphor embodies a number of assumptions:

- That every observed effect has a previous observable cause.
- That even the most complicated things can be understood by breaking down the whole into its component parts and then analysing them.
- The focus is on the particular characteristics of the parts.
- A change in one part only affects those other parts which are immediately close to it – the 'knock-on' effect.
- That if we analyse past events sufficiently, this will then help us to both predict and control future events.
- The intelligence of organisations resides in the minds of those who design and redesign them.

Much of the language of leadership and management then reflects this machine orientation – terms like 'structure', 'design', 'tools', 'techniques', 'standardisation', 'routines', 'specifications', 'step up a gear', 'run like clockwork', 'like a well-oiled machine', 'levers', 'policy instruments' and 're-engineering', for example. This indicates the extent to which these describing and working in organisations have been seduced by the machine metaphor and have internalised both the language and the related way of thinking. It is important, for example, to remember that any system does not map neatly onto an organisation chart, which is essentially only a machine blueprint. As has been stated, 'The map is not the territory it represents' (Korzbski, 1959).

Moreover:

- People in organisations do not necessarily just obey the instructions that they are given. Instead they think, react and interpret. As someone once said 'With every pair of hands you also get a brain'.
- People often make quite different assumptions and so have conflicting views and perspectives on the same thing.

- People have different ways of making sense of the world.
- The context varies, depending on such factors as culture, previous history, allegiance and aspiration.

The major emerging alternative view is that:

- Human (social) systems are actually living systems and so cannot be controlled, measured or fixed as if they were machines.
- Such systems are complex, unpredictable and are thus constantly evolving and adapting.
- Different parts of a system are connected and are interdependent – so relationships and connections between the parts really do matter.

So instead, and alternatively, organisations individually and collectively can be conceived as *complex adaptive systems*, based on a quite different metaphor – that of living systems. A system is simply a set of things that are inter-connected in ways that produce distinct patterns of behaviour. It is the relationships between the individual parts that give rise to their emergent behaviour. A complex adaptive system is described as:

> A dynamic network of agents acting in parallel, constantly reacting to what the other agents are doing, which in turn influences behaviour and the network as a whole. Control tends to be dispersed and decentralised and the overall behaviour of the system is the result of many decisions made constantly by individual agents. Order emerges rather than being predetermined. It is not possible to reverse the system's history and the future is often unpredictable.
>
> *(Holland, 1999)*

Thus, the characteristics of complex adaptive systems include:

- A large number of parts or elements which interact together dynamically. They 'hang together' and continually affect each other over time, so the focus is on the relationship between the parts, rather than the parts themselves. Complex adaptive systems are 'messy' webs that are constantly shifting and involve tangible things (like people and organisations) interwoven with intangible things (like context and culture).
- A history whereby the past helps to shape present behaviour. In fact, today's problems often have their origins in yesterday's solutions.
- Openness, so it may be difficult to exactly define system boundaries.
- Interactions are non-linear because cause and effect are distant in time and space with the area of a system generating problems often being distant from the area showing the symptoms.
- The different parts of the system are not aware of the behaviour of the system as a whole and respond only to what information is available or known locally. Everyone who is part of a system holds a different perspective on its nature, purpose and boundaries. No-one can see the whole picture about how to make change happen

because the system looks quite different depending upon where you are situated within it. So to understand the system as a whole you need multiple perspectives from different angles, because no one person or group holds the whole truth.

- Everything and everyone in the system exists in relationships, and relationships involve emotions.
- Even small changes can have large effects, but the areas of highest leverage are often the least obvious.
- A constant flow of energy to maintain the organisation of the system.
- Order emerges 'for free' – the system does exactly what it is designed to do.

They also have a range of properties, which are:

Emergence: Change emerges from the way the whole system behaves, not from the actions of any one organisation, project or programme. The agents in the system interact in apparently random and non-linear ways, but from all of these interactions patterns emerge which ultimately inform and change the behaviour of the agents and of the system itself. So a system is relatively stable and 'stuff gets done' – so complexity results in order, rather than disorder, despite the 'mess'.

Co-evolution: Systems are part of a broader environment and most systems are embedded within other systems, so as the environment changes, systems also change in order to ensure best fit with it. This in turn influences the wider environment and creates a constant cycle of change as the system develops to adapt to the environment and the environment changes as a result of system alterations.

Connectivity: How agents in a system connect and relate to one other is critical to the system's survival and so the relationships between the agents are usually seen as more important than the agents themselves. There are always unintended consequences and all attempts to manage these consequences add even more complexity (and even more unintended consequences).

Iteration: Small changes within a system can build like a snowball rolling downhill, leading to larger change.

Requisite variety: The greater the variety within the system, the stronger it will be, and the more likely it will be able to create new possibilities and to co-evolve.

Self-organising: There is no hierarchy of command – no central command-and-control mechanism. Complex adaptive systems are constantly reorganising themselves to find the best fit with their environment. The past (and the cultural practices which it embodies) has shaped the present, holding a system into its existing patterns. If the environment changes then the system in turn needs to adapt.

Edge of chaos: The most productive optimum state for a system is at the 'edge of chaos' where there is maximum variety, creativity and adaptability. Here the system is sufficiently structured to carry information about itself and to perform tasks adequately and, at the same time, sufficiently chaotic to allow it to use that information creatively. It is the balance between vitality on the one hand and robustness and resilience on the other.

Simple rules: Complex adaptive systems are not complicated and can often be governed by a set of simple principles. For example, Obolensky (2014) suggests that these might include:

- An underlying purpose.
- A clear boundary.
- A tolerance for uncertainty and ambiguity.
- Clear personal objectives.
- Continuous feedback.
- Discretion and freedom of action.
- The skill and will of participants.

Regarding health and social care as a local complex adaptive system is the approach taken in this book.

The nature of health and social care organisations

The governance arrangements for health and social care organisations are different in the different parts of the UK. In England, Wales and Scotland health care organisations are ultimately accountable to Government Ministers and Parliaments/ Assemblies while social care is largely provided by or facilitated by local authorities which are made up of elected councillors, often leading to charges from local government that health care suffers from a local 'democratic deficit'. The exception is Northern Ireland where health and social care were organisationally united in the 1970s and are accountable to the Northern Ireland Assembly (when it operates).

The NHS is largely free at the point of use, while local authorities typically only pay for individual packages of care for adults assessed as having high needs and limited means. Additionally, many care homes and other social care services are typically located in the private sector, sometimes having previously been supplied by statutory health and social care organisations. There is thus a complex range of organisations, professionals and services. The boundaries between the organisations concerned and between the roles of key staff have become ever more fluid and permeable as jobs and teams that were once separate are often merged and sometimes de-merged.

Unsurprisingly, therefore, there are major barriers to effective joint working and integration between health and social care organisations and to considerations of them as a single local system. In no particular order they include:

- The geographical areas over which health and local government services are planned and delivered often do not align, which can make it difficult for the relevant organisations and their staff to come together to support integrated care.
- A lack of a clear overall shared vision and purpose for services, people and the local community on the part of the major stake-holding partners. No single shared 'narrative' exists covering the entire system, meaning that those

differences or gaps which need to be addressed either are unrecognised or are unresolved.

- National bureaucratic restraints to pursuing changes to the local status quo, as local silos are replicated in national Government departments and vice versa. These policy silos result in inconsistent commissioning, funding and regulatory processes, all of which operate according to different geographies, timescales, rules, regulations and targets.
- In England the Health and Social Care Act of 2012, which was designed primarily to promote competition, has imposed constraints and transaction costs that limit the integration of services for the benefit of service users and divert resources away from service delivery and towards management processes.
- Private companies account for the vast majority of provision of adult social care in both the care home and homecare markets. The collapse of some providers, the handing-back of contracts to local authorities and well-publicised scandals all reveal the fragility of the model (Hudson, 2018).
- In Northern Ireland, the on-off existence of the Assembly limits the political will to develop a consistent policy direction for health and social care.
- Different and often confusing national inspectorial and regulatory frameworks and regimes and major difficulties in being really open and honest with regard to 'scandals' and 'failures'. A tendency, perhaps, to blame scapegoats – individual 'bad apples', rather than systemic failures
- A culture of short-termism and reactive stop-go approaches, often in response to national policy initiatives. Central government has typically had unrealistic expectations of the pace at which any required changes in working practices can progress. There is often therefore political pressure to make demonstrable change quickly, while in practice it takes a long time for effective (rather than cosmetic) change to develop and hence to demonstrate real transformation. There is therefore a constant challenge for local organisations trying to deliver long-term, cross-cutting outcomes within the constraints of short-term budgets and frequently changing policy requirements. Short-term funding cycles also risk perpetuating a costly bidding culture in which local areas can spend more time and money putting together bids for different funding pots from central government, rather than building the necessary capability to work together as a local system.
- Education and training for the major professions concerned – medicine, nursing and social work – largely being conducted separately. A lack of continuing and sustained investment in the training and development activity which is directed towards joint working and integration.
- Confusion with regard to the role and intentions of the voluntary, charitable and community sectors – are they primarily about advocacy, operational delivery of services, being a representative of service users or contributing strategically, or what possible combination of those?
- Different staff remuneration structures and terms and conditions of employment between health and social care.

- While 1.3 million people work in the NHS in England alone, there are 1.8 million people employed in social care (Kearney, 2018), 75% of them in front-line care roles. More than a quarter of the social care workforce leave every year, fostering a growing dependence on agency staff (Gershlich et al., 2017). The two workforces are very different. The health care workforce is characterised by a high degree of professional specialism, with undergraduate education being the starting-point for most entrants. The vast majority of social care workers, by contrast, are not registered professionals and will have earned vocational qualifications whilst in work. However, around a quarter of the health care workforce is made up of Health Care Assistants and their training is neither compulsory nor consistent, and social workers do constitute a university-qualified profession within social care.
- Creating an integrated health and social care workforce is inhibited by the existing difficulties in recruiting and retaining such staff, particularly in community and domiciliary care.
- A lack of understanding of the particular pressures which are faced by the other organisations in the system.
- Different decision-making processes in operation in different organisations, especially in terms of the levels of delegated authority in place in order to make particular decisions.
- A lack of focus on the possibilities of longer-term approaches beyond the bounds of current traditional organisational and professional roles.
- Difficulty in having truly open and honest conversations about what might need to change in the face of exposure to constant political and media scrutiny.
- A lack of clarity over different professional and managerial roles and responsibilities, which leads towards a blame culture.
- Stereotyping of potential partners. Health care organisations often view local government as short-termist and driven by the prevailing political mood, while some in local government see the NHS as something of a leviathan that lacks democratic accountability, is politically naïve, and is out of touch with local communities.
- Separate budgets and different financial regimes, combined with scarce and diminishing financial resources. There are many misaligned financial incentives that work against sharing such resources and risks. These arise in part from the difference between the separate health and social care financing arrangements, the former being free at the point of delivery and based only on clinical need (with, in England, costs for acute care calculated on a tariff or episode basis) and the latter rationed by means-testing. The number of people eligible for local authority social care has reduced in the face of funding cuts. Most social care provision is now obtained through the private and not for profit sectors and the links between these providers and NHS organisations have not always been strong. Additionally, payment systems in the NHS (especially in England) have promoted competition and driven activity in hospitals. Short-term, sporadic and ad-hoc funding allocated in order to react to short-term pressures and concerns regarding the possibilities of 'cost-shunting' between organisations are also major factors.

- Additional funding for health and social care has, at times, been used to address the immediate need to reduce service and financial pressures in the acute health sector. Current accountability arrangements, set by legislation, emphasise the need for individual organisations to balance their books. Funding constraints can sometimes incentivise competition over collaboration as organisations may see each other as rivals for limited funds. Constrained budgets also mean that organisations may be reluctant to support programmes that produce savings for other parts of the local system, without direct benefits for themselves, especially where high up-front costs are likely to only produce savings in the long term. Moreover, some health and social care organisations face challenges of organisational viability, from shrinking budgets and overspends to staff recruitment and retention issues.
- Different performance management regimes and cultures, both in terms of organisational performance metrics and individual performance appraisal.
- Shifting organisational structures and roles due to continuing internal reorganisations leading, in turn, to dislocations in working relationships and a corresponding lack of continuity. Organisational restructuring typically serves to distract and disappoint (O'Leary & Gerard, 2012).
- Reticence problems regarding the sharing of information, including separate and incompatible IT systems; issues regarding data accuracy, robustness and timeliness; problems in aggregating different versions of the same data and a general reluctance to share data. A tension between the need to share relevant information and issues of service user/patient confidentiality. These problems with sharing data across health and social care can prevent an individual's care from being coordinated smoothly.
- A lack of co-location of health and social care services. Territorial issues, including the sharing of property and equipment.
- A lack of leadership, management and staff capacity which leads to a culture of overwork, to stress and to 'initiative fatigue' as many people often feel that they are 'running to stand still'. It may thus be difficult to motivate staff due to their previous experience with other initiatives and pilots.
- Cultures of 'not invented here' and hence an inability or unwillingness to learn from others. Lessons and experience are not systematically shared, not least because there are limited incentives to evaluate programmes and activity in a rigorous manner and to spread the conclusions.
- Vested professional and managerial interests who fiercely guard their independence for its own sake, together with people who do not separate their own personal position from that of their employing organisations – and so seek to defend both. People hang on to power sometimes even in the face of being presented with the means to do things better. It is not that they don't want to do good – but they also don't want to lose their power.
- Perceived power differentials and status differences between various professional staff. This is often associated with a lack of understanding with regard to the professional roles of others and thus to related inter-professional mistrust, often associated with concern over the erosion of professional role boundaries.

- The use of intra-professional language and specialist jargon and acronyms, leading to obfuscation of meaning. The exact same words can, for example, potentially mean quite different things to different professional audiences.

- Professional territoriality, often labelled as 'tribalism' where each profession has a different culture, which includes values, beliefs, attitudes, customs, codes of practice and behaviours and which has evolved as the professions have developed, reflecting historical factors, as well as class and gender issues. Educational experiences and the socialisation process that occurs during professional education and training serve to reinforce the common values, problem-solving approaches and language/jargon of each profession. So for many people, their personal and professional identity is bound up with the way things currently are; is manifested in traditions, symbols, rituals, language, stories and practices, so any threat to the status quo is experienced as a personal and professional threat to themselves. People who have spent their entire careers working towards delivering a specific set of goals and statutory duties, undertaking a specific set of activities and developing specific ways of working inevitably will therefore have varying levels of appetite for greater collaboration. They may feel threatened by new models of care, be risk averse and so be reluctant to embrace new ways of working. Evidence suggests that the existence of such strong boundaries between professional groups serves to slow the spread of innovation (Ferlie et al., 2005).

- A special case of this tribalism may be related to General Practice and there are various reasons for this, including legitimate concerns about quality, accountability and governance issues in relation to more integrated working; a lack of capacity to attend the relevant engagement activities and events needed and with some GPs viewing integration as a threat to their independent practice.

Underlying such tensions may be different perspectives derived from the medical model of care and the psycho-social model of care. The former focuses especially upon the individual's health, adopting a bio-medical approach. It places an emphasis upon professional expertise and on 'fixing' conditions, through rapid assessment (diagnosis) and treatment. It is best expressed thus:

> People are healthy until they fall ill. Illness is caused by a disease which is usually an invasion of the body by a poison, a germ or an accident. Ill people go to doctors who study their signs and symptoms and diagnose the disease. They then apply treatments, medications, surgery or special regimes which cure the disease, mend the injury, drive out the poison or kill the germs. Some illnesses can be cured at home but for some it is necessary to go into hospital. There the doctors carry out their tests and later their treatments while the nurses provide care, make the patient comfortable and carry out the doctors' orders. Hospitals are basically places in which patients are cured by the doctors' skill and cared for by the nurses.

> *(Clark, 1974)*

The latter adopts a social and contextual approach, where the family and sets of relationships are important and where the relationship with the service user is key. Such an approach accepts that there may be multiple causes for particular conditions and that there may be ambiguity about such causes. It is also strongly concerned with empowering the service user.

Nonetheless, there are also major similarities, particularly for the front-line professional staff working in health and social care because they have to undertake what has been called 'emotional labour'. Emotional labour is a fairly recent term used to describe a much older phenomenon. Revans (1964), for example, at an early stage in the 1960s described the hospital as an institution 'cradled in anxiety' and Menzies Lyth (1959) highlighted health care staff as bearing 'the full immediate and concentrated impact of distress, tragedy, death and dying which arise from patient care and which are not part of the typical working experience for most of the public', while Tallis (2005) identified that:

> It is easy to forget the appalling nature of some of the jobs carried out by health care staff day-in, day-out – the damage, the pain, the mess they may encounter, the sheer stench of diseased human flesh and its waste products …

and that:

> Contact with emotional distress and disturbance can be harrowing. Existential questions about identity, suffering, madness and death are raised and may put people in touch with extreme feelings of confusion, pain and loss. The struggle with feelings of helplessness and hopelessness in the face of suffering cannot be avoided and individuals, depending on their personality and past experience, protect themselves in different ways from the emotionally traumatic environment.

Emotional labour is therefore defined as the 'suppression of feeling in order to sustain an outward appearance that produces in others a sense of being cared for' (Hayward & Tuckey, 2011). In practice it involves:

- The depersonalisation and categorisation of users of services.
- The cultivation of professional detachment and self-control – a 'caring but distant' demeanour.
- Ritualistic task performance involving checking, rechecking and form-filling used as a means of avoidance.
- Delegation of decisions upwards to more senior staff in order to avoid the taking-on of personal responsibility for them.
- A suspicion of change – or alternatively an obsession with regular reorganisations.

The protection against that anxiety which care-giving induces by the suppression of personal emotions over a sustained time-period leads eventually to a reduced ability to withstand the emotional toll of care which, in turn, leads to either emotional burn-out or to an unhealthy detachment – a state which involves no longer noticing or acting on the distress of others.

While this is particularly true of individual health care workers, as many 'scandals' have revealed, there is also an organisational impact:

> Health care organisations operate in society as 'containers' of the emotions and anxieties of patients' relatives and families and because of this the experience of leaders and managers of clinical professional staff is different from that of an industrial/commercial enterprise. Managerial initiatives from the 1980s onwards have served to increase and bolster the potential defence mechanisms in play to deal with the inherent anxiety of working in health care. Increased bureaucratisation of professional work has also served to increase prescription and decrease discretion.
>
> *(Edmonstone, 2013)*

Although the focus of the growing number of studies of emotional labour has largely been confined to health care staff and organisations, the phenomenon clearly also exists in social care professions and organisations (Case, 2018). A move away from relationship-based social work towards case management in the 1990s, for example, has seen managerialism, procedures and bureaucracy become the social work raison d'être. The Munro (2011) review highlighted:

- The emphasis on complying with prescription and with the keeping of records in order to demonstrate compliance, at the expense of forming and cultivating relationships with service users.
- That high levels of prescription had hampered the social work profession's ability to take responsibility for developing its own knowledge and skills.
- The priority given to process over practice had led to insufficient attention being given as to whether service users actually benefited from the services which they received.

Moreover, both health care and social care organisations have historically been hierarchical in nature, with a predominant 'command-and-control' culture of bureaucratic direction and regulation. Front-line health and social care staff have previously been described as 'street level bureaucrats' with a degree of discretion with regard to how they enact the policies which are assigned to them to uphold (Lipsky, 1980). However, there is growing evidence that over time such discretion has increasingly been eroded (Wastell et al., 2010; Ellis, 2011). In social work, for example, as the Munro review emphasised, it is clear that problem-solving has become increasingly formulaic, procedural and drawn into managerialism and bureaucracy (Abbott & Taylor, 2013).

Approaches to developing health and social care organisations

There are effectively three approaches to the development of health and social care organisations. They are:

- Intra-organisational
- Inter-organisational
- Co-evolutionary.

Intra-organisational

Here the development focus is internally within a single organisation and the emphasis is on current and anticipated future challenges and the interventions which are needed to address them, as a single organisational agenda is pursued. Typically, such challenges would include such areas as fostering a more integrated corporate identity; the development of strategic planning and performance management; the enhancement of internal communication and engagement strategies; the identification and development of leadership and management competence and of talent management and succession planning frameworks.

Inter-organisational

This involves bi-lateral and multi-lateral co-ordination and co-operation across health and social care organisations in order to achieve shared goals or outcomes and is likely to build upon any already existing inter-organisational relationships and also to require new bi-lateral and multi-lateral activity. Greater inter-organisational co-ordination and co-operation are needed in order to reduce duplication, to add value, to pool resources and generally to fit the pieces of the 'jigsaw' better together. This can centre around a particular client group ('horizontal integration') or through a delivery chain ('vertical integration').

The underlying assumption is that an organisation is primarily motivated by its own self-interest, but there will also be situations where co-operation is a better strategy than competition. The goals may be peculiar to a single organisation, but the partners see their future as being linked in some way. They therefore act to influence the behaviour of the other organisation(s) over time because, instead of the win/lose of competition, there is the possibility of a win/win relationship. It has also (and somewhat mischievously) been called 'the sublimation of loathing in the pursuit of funding' (Middleton, 2007)!

The overall intentions of this approach are:

- To promote improved trust and communication between the organisations concerned.
- To help to enlarge the 'shadow of the future'. A serious barrier to the evolution of co-operation in organisational life is the lack of continuity of

relationships from the past, through the present, and into the future. If there is frequent job movement then there is little opportunity for the iterative interactions with others that are required in order to foster co-operation. Moreover, if people and organisations do not expect to have to keep working together (or can see such relationships as being time-limited) then the incentives to co-operate tend to decay rapidly. Fostering such co-operation therefore requires a degree of stability in those relationships, avoiding unnecessary organisational restructuring and even building expectations regarding the length of stay in post of key people.

- To create those internal organisational policies and procedures that reward co-operation and long-term behaviour.
- To encourage the organisations concerned to make their internal decision-making processes as consistent and transparent as possible.
- To allow and encourage staff to interact mainly with others in the other organisations who also use co-operative strategies.

In reviewing such inter-organisational development the notion of 'collaborative advantage' has been coined, as an alternative to the better-known concept of competitive advantage (Huxham & Vangen, 2005). The suggestions about how to make collaborative advantage work include:

- Don't do it unless you have to! Joint working with other organisations is inherently both difficult and resource-consuming. Unless the potential for real collaborative advantage can be seen, it is probably most efficient to operate unilaterally.
- Budget a great deal more time for the collaborative activities than you would normally expect to need.
- Remember that the other participants involved are unlikely to want to achieve exactly the same thing as you and so make allowances. Protect your own agendas but also be prepared to compromise.
- Where possible, try to begin by setting out with some small and achievable tasks. Build up mutual trust gradually through achieving mutual small wins. Alternatively, if the stakes are high, a more comprehensive trust-building approach may be needed.
- Pay attention to communication. Be aware of your own organisational and professional jargon and try to find clear ways to express ideas to others who do not share your daily world. If partners speak in ways that do not make sense, do not be afraid to ask for clarification.
- Do not expect other organisations to do things exactly the same way as yours does. Things that may be easy to do in your organisation may, for example, be difficult and so require major political manoeuvring in another.
- Ensure that those who have to manage the collaboration are briefed to be able to act with an appropriate degree of autonomy and discretion. Wherever

possible, they need to be able to react quickly and contingently without having to check back to their 'parent' organisation.

- Recognise that power plays can often be a part of the negotiation process Both understanding your own power sources and ensuring that the partner organisations do not feel vulnerable can be a valuable part of building trust.
- Understand that making things happen involves acting in both facilitative *and* directive ways towards others.
- Assume that you cannot be wholly in control and that your partners and the context in which you and they operate will be continually changing.

One of the dangers of this approach is that of 'partnership fatigue' because the benefits of struggling to work together are not always clear to see. Obviously many of these suggestions also apply to the co-evolutionary approach described below which has been typified as systems leadership, but the emphasis in systems leadership is much less calculative and instrumental in nature and is strongly focused on service users and communities.

Co-evolutionary (or learning together into the future)

The methods which are applicable in terms of inter-organisational working (such as project management) now become less helpful, as the focus is now not on past patterns and activities that are known to work or about co-ordinating known good practice, but instead about working and learning together into the future, which is, of course, not yet knowable. The time-frame is therefore necessarily long and the collective goal less clearly-defined than the objectives of inter-organisational working. The necessary conditions for co-evolution are (Harries et al., 1999):

- *Building relationships:* People need time in order to be able to explore purpose. Sufficient numbers of people need to understand exactly why they are working together in partnership and what this means in practice.
- *Changing mental maps:* The mind-set of those involved needs to change so that people see themselves as part of a 'whole' and so reject the shifting of blame when things go wrong from one part of the health and social care system to another.
- *Diversity:* There needs to be a sufficient mix of people from different organisations and from different levels within those organisations to enable new possibilities to emerge.
- *Expectation:* That change can be fuelled by both energy and passion, and not just by money, and that common purpose can be the source of coherence.
- *Iteration:* People need to be able to try and try again. One-off and single project-based activity is simply not enough.
- *Responsibility:* The leadership task is to create conditions so that people can take responsibility for the behaviour of the 'whole' as well as their own independent behaviour.

- *Future:* Incentives which enlarge the shadow of the future and enable people to see that their futures are linked are needed.

The differences between these development approaches are shown in Table 1.4.

A co-evolutionary approach now entails the adoption of systems leadership because single organisations can no longer respond effectively to the wicked issues which they face unless they work collectively and across the system (Checkland, 1999). Single organisations have neither the people nor the finance needed to respond to the current and anticipated future levels of expectation, nor do they singly possess sufficient know-how required to address complex and multi-dimensional problems, unless they pool their intelligence, skills and information. It implies an entirely new way of thinking about the leadership required to explain what is happening and to learn from practice. There is a huge leap between collaborating through self-interest and working in the interests of the system first and the employing organisation second, and this requires a shift in mind-set, culture and behaviour.

The 'system' is rarely any single organisation, sector or even the public agencies associated with one place. It can also involve a wide range of commercial and not-for-profit organisations and a complex web of people. The idea that these will conform to a model of leadership based on a single organisational model with hierarchical power structures is simply not sustainable. Traditional organisational leadership models and their associated behaviours do not stand up in this environment, so there is a need for leaders to shift their focus from loyalty to their organisation towards the citizen as service user and the wider population – in other words towards the system.

TABLE 1.4 Three ways of working

	Intra-organisational	*Inter-organisational*	*Systems Leadership*
Vision of the system	A single-organisation perception	A shared commitment to improve the system	A means to develop new possibilities and ways of working
Nature of partnership	Working to own rules, with occasional partnership activity	Time-limited or similar cooperative projects	A journey, not a destination; a matter of degree, not an end-state
Use of resources	To meet own organisation's objectives	To meet complementary objectives; mutual reinforcement	To meet system objectives in a creative way
Decision-making	Independent	Consultative	Co-designed for a shared purpose
Information	Used independently	Circulates between partners on the basis of agreed protocols	An information-rich environment

Systems leadership

Systems leadership is leadership within and across organisational and geopolitical boundaries, beyond individual professional disciplines, involving a range of organisational and stakeholder cultures, often without direct managerial control of resources and working on issues of mutual concern that cannot be addressed by any one person or agency. It seeks to affect change for social good through multiple interacting and intersecting services. It can be contrasted with intra-organisational and inter-organisational leadership approaches based upon direct, positional or hierarchical authority (often referred to as 'command-and-control') which are less effective in the circumstances that most public service leaders now face, which are best addressed through non-linear and emergent leadership approaches.

It is about the way people need to behave when they face large, complex, difficult and seemingly intractable wicked problems; where they need to juggle the multiple uncertainties which they face; where no one person or organisation can find or organise a way forward on their own; where everyone is grappling with how to make the existing resources meet the demand which is outstripping them; and where the way forward therefore lies in involving as many people's energies, ideas, talents and expertise as possible. Once ambiguous issues are addressed, understanding of the complexity of the problems increases and the number of stakeholders involved, from many different areas and backgrounds, starts to rise. Such messy and complex issues are simply too hard for individuals or single organisations alone to fully comprehend or manage.

It is certainly significantly more than working inter-organisationally – more than mutually-beneficial joint working or collaboration, as it involves a co-evolved or co-created agenda and practice. Service users are at the core of systems leadership, which is a collective activity – done with others and not alone. It is a form of 'distributed' leadership which permeates the system at all levels and not just at the top of organisational hierarchies. It assumes that leadership is not a position, but a behaviour that can show up anywhere. It is what happens when people step forward to make a difference for the issues that they care about, whether or not they have positional power and expertise. It is empowering, rather than 'heroic' and involves ceding, not grabbing or appropriating power. It is about earning legitimacy with ideas and actions that resonate, so that people willingly grant authority to systems leaders. It is fully-focused on outcomes for service users and communities, rather than the elegance of organisational design or of professional boundaries. It is concerned with credibility and with influencing through 'nudges', rather than with command-and-control, and this is necessary in situations where authority might not be recognised and where control of resources lies outwith a single organisation. It is not about quick wins and takes a lot of time to achieve results. It rather involves a 'long game' and is an attempt to effect change for the social good across those multiple interacting and intersecting services. It is a mind-set or way of thinking, rather than specific actions and behaviours.

Systems leadership is characterised by two key attributes. Firstly, it is a collective form of leadership – 'leadership as participation', rather than 'leadership as performance', because it involves the concerted effort of many people working together at different places in the system and at different levels, rather than single leaders acting unilaterally. Secondly, systems leadership crosses boundaries, both physical, organisational, professional and virtual and therefore extends individual leaders well beyond the usual limits of the formal responsibilities and authority that are located within their employing organisations.

Systems leadership is highly relevant for people involved in the delivery of health and social care services, especially in relation to the challenge of integrating such complex services around individual service users and communities. The aim is to transcend sectional organisational interests and work together on the basis of shared ambition, with a view to making progress towards better health and wellbeing outcomes across a population. It is less of a 'nice to have' and more of a 'must have'. It is, however, about exploration and it may not be possible at the outset to know exactly what the way forward is, what the route or routes to be followed are or when you will know that you have arrived. This is, of course, counter-cultural and therefore very challenging.

It involves working in a system and, at the same time, acting as a change agent within that system in order to develop and improve provision to service users and the communities in which they live and work. That said, systems leadership is obviously not easy, is definitely not some silver bullet panacea and will certainly not solve all problems. It cannot compensate for poorly-managed or under-resourced services, nor can it 'magic up' new resources – and it is certainly not about toolkits or 'top tips'. However, it has rightly been called 'the difference that makes the difference' (Bolden et al., 2015). It is a marker of a more general shift in the modes of transmission from hierarchical to viral, and, in forms of social organisation, from analogue to digital. Arguably, it is the only kind of leadership that is likely to survive the advent of social media.

To emulate those people who have been successful in leading in complex systems, the following approaches have been highlighted (Welbourn et al., 2012):

- Always go out of your way to make new connections.
- Adopt an open and enquiring mind-set, refusing to be constrained at all by the current horizons.
- Embrace uncertainty and ambiguity and be positive about change – adopt an entrepreneurial attitude.
- Draw upon as many different perspectives as is possible; diversity is non-optional.
- Ensure that leadership and decision-making are distributed throughout all levels and functions.
- Establish a compelling vision which is shared by all the stakeholders across the whole system.
- Promote the importance of values – invest as much energy into relationships and behaviours as into delivering tasks.

This chapter has shown that there has been a necessary journey away from using the machine metaphor in thinking about and working with organisations and towards seeing organisations instead as complex adaptive systems. The need now is to regard health and social care – and all the organisations, agencies, charities, professions and groups contained therein, as a single local system. The point is not whether doing so and emphasising the need for systems leadership is 'real' or not, only whether it agrees with what is increasingly observed in practice. As such, it represents a form of 'model-dependent realism' (Hawking & Mlodinow, 2011) – a mental model created in order to interpret, understand and work in the everyday world.

References

Abbott, C. & Taylor, P. (2013) *Action Learning in Social Work*, London: Sage

Ballatt, J. & Campling, P. (2011) *Intelligent Kindness: Reforming the Culture of Healthcare*, London: RCPsych Publications

Bolden, R., Gulati, A., Ahmad, Y., Burgoyne, J., Chapman, N., Edwards, G., Green, E., Owen, D., Smith, I. & Spirit, M. (2015) *The Difference that Makes the Difference: Final Evaluation of the First Place-Based Programme for Systems Leadership: Local Vision*, Bristol: University of the West of England

Bolden, R., Witzel, M. & Linacre, N. (2016) *Leadership Paradoxes: Leadership for an Uncertain World*, Abingdon: Routledge

Broughton, A., Gloster, R., Marvell, R., Green, M., Langley, J. & Martin, A. (2018) *The Experiences of Individuals in the Gig Economy*, Brighton: Institute for Employment Studies, for Department for Business, Energy & Industrial Strategy

Case, P. (2018) Care Workers Need Support to Handle the Emotional Impact of our Jobs, *Guardian*, 13 February

Checkland, P. (1999) *Systems Thinking, Systems Practice*, Chichester: Wiley

Clark, D. (1974) *Social Therapy in Psychiatry*, London: Pelican

Edmonstone, J. (2011) The Challenge of Capability in Leadership Development, *British Journal of Healthcare Management*, 17(12): 541–547

Edmonstone, J. (2013) What Is Wrong with NHS Leadership Development? *British Journal of Healthcare Management*, 19(11): 531–538

Ellis, K. (2011) 'Street Level Bureaucracy' Revisited: The Changing Face of Frontline Discretion in Adult Social Care in England, *Social Policy Administration*, 45(3): 221–244

Eraut, M. (1994) *Developing Professional Knowledge and Competence*, London: Falmer Press

Ferlie, E., Fitzgerald, L., Wood, M. & Hawkins, C. (2005) The Non-Spread of Innovations: The Mediating Role of Professionals, *Academy of Management Journal*, 48(1): 117–134

Gershlich, B., Charlesworth, A., Thorlby, R. & Jones, H. (2017) *A Sustainable Workforce: The Lifeblood of the NHS and Social Care*, London: The Health Foundation

Global Future (2018) *10,000 Carers Missing: How Ending Free Movement Could Spell Disaster for Elderly and Disabled People*, London: Global Future

Grint, K. (2008) Wicked Problems and Clumsy Solutions: The Role of Leadership, *Clinical Leader*, 1(2): 54–68

Harries, J., Gordon, P., Plamping, D. & Fischer, M. (1999) *Elephant Problems and Fixes that Fail: The Story of a Search for New Approaches to Inter-Agency Working*, London: King's Fund

Hawking, S. & Mlodinow, L. (2011) *The Grand Design*, London: Bantam Press

Hayward, R. and Tuckey, M. (2011) Emotions in Uniform: How Nurses Regulate Emotions at Work via Emotional Boundaries, *Human Relations*, 64(11): 1501–1523

Heifetz, R., Grashow, A. & Linsky, M. (2009) *The Practice of Adaptive Leadership: Tools and Tactics for Changing your Organisation and the World*, Boston: Harvard Business Publishing

Holland, J. (1999) *Emergence: From Chaos to Order*, Reading, Mass.: Perseus Books

Hudson, B. (2018) The Only Way Is Ethics: A New Approach to Outsourcing Social Care, *Guardian*, 20 August

Huxham, C. & Vangen, S. (2005) *Managing to Collaborate: The Theory and Practice of Collaborative Advantage*, Abingdon: Routledge

Kearney, J. (2018) *The Economic Value of the Adult Social Care Sector UK*, London: ICF Consulting for Skills for Care and Development

Korzbski, A. (1959) *Science and Sanity: An Introduction to Non-Aristotelian Systems and General Semantics*, Forest Hills, NY: Institute of General Semantics

Lipsky, M. (1980) *Street Level Bureaucracy: Dilemmas of the Individual in Public Services*, New York, NY: Russell Sage Foundation

Mencken, H. (1982) *A Mencken Chrestomathy*, New York: First Vintage Books

Menzies Lyth, I. (1959) The Functioning of Social Systems as a Defence Against Anxiety: A Report on a Study of the Nursing Service of a General Hospital, in Menzies Lyth, I. (1988) *Containing Anxiety in Institutions: Selected Essays: Volume 1*, London: Free Association Books, pp. 43–88

Middleton, J. (2007) *Beyond Authority: Leadership in a Changing World*, Basingstoke: Palgrave Macmillan

Morgan, G. (1986) *Images of Organisations*, London: Sage Publications

Munro, E. (2011) *The Munro Review of Child Protection: Final Report: A Child Centred System*, London: The Stationery Office

Obolensky, N. (2014) *Complex Adaptive Leadership: Embracing Paradox and Uncertainty* (2nd edition), Farnham: Gower Publishing

OECD (2018) *A Broken Elevator?: How to Promote Social Mobility*, Paris: Organisation for Economic Co-operation and Development

O'Leary, C. & Gerard, C. (2012) The Skills Set of the Successful Collaborator, *Public Administration Review*, 72(1): 70–83

Peston, R. (2017) *WTF?*, London: Hodder & Stoughton

Peter, L. & Hull, R. (1969) *The Peter Principle: Why Things Always Go Wrong*, New York: William Morrow & Co.

Plsek, P. & Greenhalgh, T. (2001) The Challenge of Complexity in Health Care, *British Medical Journal* 323(7313): 625–658

Raworth, K. (2017) *Doughnut Economics: Seven Ways to Think Like a 21st Century Economist*, London: Random House Business Books

Revans, R. (1964) *Standards for Morale: Cause and Effect in Hospitals*, Oxford: Oxford University Press

Rittell, H. & Webber, M. (1973) Dilemmas in a General Theory of Planning, *Policy Sciences*, 4: 155–169

Sarason, S. (1978) The Nature of Problem-Solving in Social Action, *American Psychologist*, 33 (4): 370–380

Stacey, R. (2002) *Strategic Management and Organisational Dynamics: The Challenge of Complexity*, Harlow: Prentice-Hall

Standing, G. (2011) *The Precariat: The Dangerous New Class*, London: Policy Network

Tallis, R. (2005) *Hippocratic Oaths: Medicine and its Discontents*, London: Atlantic Books

Till, A., Dutta, N., & McKimm, J. (2016) Vertical Leadership in Highly Complex and Unpredictable Health Systems, *British Journal of Hospital Medicine*, 77(8): 471–475

Wastell, D., White, S., Broadhurst, K., Peckover, S. & Pithouse, A. (2010) Children's Services in the Iron Cage of Performance Management: Street Level Bureaucracy and the Spectre of Svejkism, *International Journal of Social Welfare*, 19(3): 310–320

Welbourn, D., Warwick, R., Carnall, C. & Fathers, D. (2012) *Leadership of Whole Systems*, London: King's Fund

Wilkinson, R. & Pickett, K. (2018) *The Inner Level: How More Equal Societies Reduce Stress, Restore Sanity and Improve Everyone's Well-Being*, London: Allen Lane

Williams, M., Broughton, A., Meager, N., Spiegelhalter, K., Johal, S. & Jenkins, K. (2017) *The True Diversity of Self-Employment*, Brighton: Centre for Research on Self-Employment; Brighton: Institute for Employment Studies

2

SYSTEMS LEADERSHIP

This chapter considers who systems leaders are, what exactly it is that systems leaders do and also identifies what an 'authorising environment' for systems leadership looks like. It describes the five 'ways' of systems leadership and locates the factors that serve to facilitate it.

Who are systems leaders?

Systems leaders are people who are involved in leading services, people, change, transformation and improvement, all of which span boundaries, which could be organisational, professional, departmental, sector and geographical – or more than likely a mix of those.

What do systems leaders do?

Systems leaders:

- View themselves as one part of an inter-connected whole. They realise that their actions form part of a web of activity which is also made up of the contributions of many others.
- Identify those challenges for which there are no obvious and ready-made technical answers and which require the gaps between values, beliefs, attitudes and behaviours to be addressed.
- Draw in those people who have different perspectives on the challenges. This involves building collaborative coalitions or alliances of different types of people. People are therefore viewed as being resourceful individuals who grow and learn from each other, rather than representatives of other organisations – resourceful humans, rather than human resources.

- Are values-driven – working in and with the health and social care system for the benefit of local communities is exactly what 'gets them up in the morning'.
- Observe the patterns that are currently existing in the wider external environment as well as those that might possibly be emerging 'over the horizon'.
- Are reflective and reflexive, demonstrating both self-knowledge and self-awareness.
- Confront, embrace and 'translate' the complexity with which they have to deal, for the benefit of others, and hence bring clarity to complex analyses. Make sense to others of what is happening by supplying for them a coherent and convincing narrative.
- Accept collective responsibility for the whole system.
- Combine constancy of purpose and resilience with a degree of flexibility and fleetness of foot.
- Conduct their business to the highest ethical standards.
- Build strong, robust and honest relationships based upon agreement around shared values, with a focus primarily on outcomes for service users, rather than just on compliance with target-based or regulatory processes.
- Demonstrate greater levels of openness – an openness of thinking (of not being limited by past assumptions); an openness in attitude (or being able to see the positive impact of a variety of perspectives); an openness in values (in order to do what's best for service users and the population), and an openness in learning (that is, being able to unlearn unhelpful past behaviours and to learn new ones more suited to a systems leadership perspective).
- Operate without the might of the hierarchy behind them and use their personal and interpersonal skills, rather than their formal organisational position, in order to achieve results. They are comfortable with ceding, rather than holding on to, power and resources.
- Focus on the personal qualities and skills of the people in the system, rather than focus on their individual competences or their grasp of techniques.
- Protect the voices of leadership across the system by ensuring that everyone's voice is heard. Engage in 'deep listening' by actively seeking out and hearing a range of diverse perspectives and challenges. Provide 'cover' for staff who may point to internal contradictions within the overall system.
- Value 'heretics' – the unorthodox thinkers who do not toe the party line and who often ask awkward questions. They can be the grit in the oyster because they can spot early potential problems that might be avoided. People can feel safe enough to ask the difficult questions, to voice disagreement and to deal with the conflict and uncomfortable emotions that may then surface.
- Maintain disciplined attention by, for example, keeping people focused, using conflict positively and watching out for possible work avoidance. Balancing patience (because it usually takes more time than envisaged to build support for change) with persistence (the determination and flexibility required to succeed) is key, as is resilience, because setbacks along the way are probably inevitable.

- Tolerate high levels of ambiguity and paradox.
- Delegate to others with appropriate empowerment to take action. Ensure that people assume responsibility and use their knowledge and experience. Support their continuing efforts by 'clearing the rocks off the runway'.
- 'Cook' any conflict which may exist, rather than avoiding it – by creating 'heat' and not flinching from difficult conversations when professional and organisational interests may conflict. This has been described as 'learning from the toxic trenches' (Gallos, 2008). It also means sequencing and pacing work activity and regulating any attendant distress.
- Allow sufficient time for *dialogue*. Dialogue emphasises the idea that meaning can flow between people and lead to a greater and shared understanding. It is best understood as an exchange of speaking and listening which is directed, not as proving one person or group right and another person wrong, but more of a process of exploration or joint inquiry. Through dialogue the hidden assumptions can be articulated, newer and deeper appreciations can be gained and unseen possibilities can be surfaced. Through being a witness to, and a participant in, a shared conversation, people can see a set of different perspectives and connections and achieve insights that are simply not possible on their own. Dialogue is therefore about emergence – the bringing forth of new and previously hidden meanings and understandings – less pre-planned and more spontaneous. Some simple rules of thumb for dialogue include:

  - *Speak well of each other.* Differences of view need to be encouraged and debated when decisions are being made.
  - *Ask, do not assume.* Not knowing is not being unprofessional, but assuming definitely is.
  - *Everyone has a role in making their voice heard and in listening to others' views and opinions,* speaking up when appropriate and giving ear to others.
  - *If we disagree or dissent, then this is done in a supportive and thoughtful way.* It is entirely possible to agree to disagree without rancour.
  - *We can only move forward if we challenge what we don't believe or agree with.* This implies being true to deeply-held values.
  - *We need to be respectful and mindful of views different from our own.* It is important to realise that there are multiple 'truths'.
  - *If in doubt, ask the service user and/or carer.* Professional staff in a wide range of organisations and roles can take a more service user-centric perspective on the design and delivery of services, engage with local community members and build a shared sense of ownership.

- Understand that a risk of failure inevitably accompanies experimentation and innovation. Systems leaders work from a basis of a degree of ignorance and even confusion with regard to issues which carry a major risk of a penalty for failure. Unless they feel that risk and are aware of what is being risked, learning from that situation is unlikely to happen. If there is no risk, then consequently there is no possibility of significant learning (Revans, 2011).

- Create a 'holding environment' – a psychological space where the addressing of wicked problems is a legitimate activity (Heifetz, 1994). This can be both a benign process of *support* (or emotional warmth) – making people feel confident and encouraging them – and also of less comfortable *challenge* to conventional ways of doing things. Support cannot simply be engineered but takes some time to build. An appropriate degree of support is often needed before any real challenge can be acceptable. This latter is likely to generate anxiety, which can have destructive or self-limiting effects, but can also potentially provide the energy which is needed in order to risk being honest, direct, challenging and different.
- One way of dealing with anxiety is the tendency to seek sanctuary in the views of experts, as such people seem to provide anxiety-reducing answers and so offer what can seem like safety and security. Yet, with complex and wicked problems such straightforward linear approaches are unlikely to work. Ways forward are more likely to come from 'lightbulb moments' which reframe the issue in ways that cross professional and organisational boundaries. The idea of a holding environment encourages ownership and focus on the issue in hand, with all the messiness, confusion and uncertainty which that entails, rather than relying upon expert advice. It encourages people to balance and to optimise the paradoxes facing them, to experiment and to develop their own ways forward, rather than simply appropriating someone else's (Edmonstone, 2017). This is shown in Figure 2.1.

That said, some systems leaders seem reluctant to claim that particular title for themselves and indeed may even see the title itself as potentially unproductive. It is, however, a phrase which has increasingly become part of the policy, organisational and professional discourse.

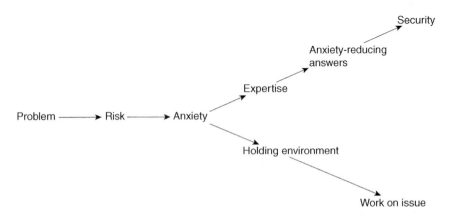

FIGURE 2.1 Alternative means of dealing with anxiety

An authorising environment for systems leadership

Systems leaders flourish best when they operate in an 'authorising environment'. Those system or organisational cultures which are based heavily on regulation or compliance with process (such as target-driven approaches) are not conducive to a culture of innovation. Rather those cultures that do foster systems leadership:

- Identify and agree on underlying values, high-level outcomes and overarching aspirations.
- Encourage both questioning and challenge.
- Recognise that positional authority is not the only source of legitimacy.
- Understand that relationships are central to leading through influence and allow for challenge and for 'difficult' conversations.
- Engender climates that enable more creative use to be made of existing resources and allow different styles of leadership to emerge and to be valued.
- Are willing to cede organisational goals for the benefit of collective ambition.
- Believe that qualities, motivations and personal styles are more important than specific competences.
- Build on local and place-based initiatives and networks.
- Display a tolerance of risk, encourage experimentation, and accept that there will be multiple pathways towards desired outcomes.
- Accept that challenge, conflict and 'disturbing' the system are all important.
- Engender the 'headspace' needed for people to think creatively, to take calculated risks, to build strong relationships and to find new ways forward.
- Share the learning that emerges from making conscientious mistakes.

The ways of systems leadership

Individual systems leaders operate through personal styles based upon (Ghate et al., 2013; Goss, 2015):

- Ways of feeling.
- Ways of perceiving.
- Ways of thinking.
- Ways of doing.
- Ways of relating.
- Ways of being.

Ways of feeling (strong personal core values)

These involve a determination to achieve better outcomes for users of services at both place-based and population levels; a belief in the value of public service and in co-operation and partnership. Such values help to transcend the individual (and sometimes competing) goals and agendas of contributing leaders and their organisations, and hence allow diverse groups to work more effectively together. They encourage people to continue with difficult work repeatedly and persistently, even when earlier attempts may have failed. As systems leadership entails risk, it is important that people really believe in what they are doing. People are unlikely to take action if they do not believe that others will do the same.

Achievement of shared values is seldom achieved in formal meetings or in formulaic ways. Systems leaders need to understand each other as people, where they come from and what they believe in. They need to be able to 'step into each other's shoes' and to discuss in depth what exactly they are trying to achieve and why. It means assessing, for example, whether the same words mean exactly the same things to each person or whether language itself offers scope for ambiguity, confusion and mistrust, because making such assumptions can potentially be dangerous. Such shared and deep conversations (which may originally commence with just a small group) help to get 'under the skin' of each partner's hopes, expectations, ways of working, beliefs and experiences and so help to build a shared understanding and confidence with regard to a joint endeavour which is likely to last for years, rather than months. These shared values also need to extend much wider and connect to the values of professional and managerial staff, service users and carers, so forging a strong sense of shared purpose.

While focusing on personal values can help to build both courage and motivation, such work may also unfortunately evoke feelings of fear, anxiety and sadness. Accessing and talking about such emotions can be important in building relationships and alliances that will be strong enough to cope with those serious difficulties which are likely to be encountered along the way.

Ways of perceiving (observations and perceptions)

These involve seeing, listening, hearing, observing, understanding and evaluating what is happening (as opposed to what might be supposed to be happening) in the system and in the surrounding context. It encompasses both having an over-arching and panoptic 'helicopter view' and cultivating a direct 'feel' for what is happening on the ground within the system, such as the arguments, the continuing personal and group attendances and absences or the protective silences. From such observation and listening it is possible to identify particular patterns of behaviour and interactions. It also involves accepting that each person or group can only see those parts of the system from their own vantage point, so some aspects of the system will remain out of view, either unseen or unknown, and thus the 'big picture' will inevitably contain elements of shadow and uncertainty that will have to be taken account of during planning and decision-making, alongside what is in plain view. What we see is what we know. We do not understand what we see, we see what we understand, and different parts of the system will care more about different outcomes. The frame of reference that we have is everything – what we see ultimately determines what we do. Having the capacity to share such viewpoints helps to build an expanded picture and so helps to identify underlying causes. This is important because:

> We all construct the world through lenses of our own making and use these to filter and select ... we need a constantly expanding array of data, views and interpretations if we are to make a wise sense of the world. We need to include more and more eyes. We need to be constantly asking 'Who else should be here?', 'Who else should be looking at this?'.
>
> *(Wheatley, 1999)*

Another way of perceiving is concerned with how the systems leader perceives his or her own role, which can switch from being a leader in some situations to being a follower in others because central to systems leadership is the perception that one's own organisational goals may often be secondary to, and even subsumed by, the wider goals of the system. A further perception is that conflict and risk can even be viewed and used creatively, rather than being 'managed out'. As Lord Rutherford is alleged to have said, while leading the Cavendish Laboratory at Cambridge University in the 1930s, 'We've got no money, so we've got to think' (Capri, 2011). The ability to seek out, and to listen attentively to, 'other voices' is also important – the teasing-out and entertaining of alternative and diverse perspectives and the welcoming of challenge and contradiction, seeing them as relevant and essential to good decision-making, rather than finding them threatening.

A danger is that a 'default position' derived from intra- and inter-organisational working is to resort to established project management approaches such as PRINCE 2, with associated work-streams, milestones and critical paths, which give a comforting illusion of progress. This may well be a form of 'avoidance activity' (Heifetz & Laurie, 1997) where what is being avoided or ignored may be the necessary hard and difficult thinking, the scary face-to-face conversations or the recognition that what is being done now simply is not working. When meetings, for example, continuously circle around the same thing without making any progress, it is highly likely that an important issue is being avoided – the proverbial 'elephant in the room'.

Ways of thinking (cognition, analysis and synthesis)

The normal public sector approach to change is to develop an overall plan or strategy, and provided that there is adequate resourcing, there can then be an implementation process. However, in working in systems, unless such plans and strategies are actually responding to what the system is doing, they become more like 'statements of intent' rather than a description of what actually happens. Plans can fail to be implemented and things can often not happen as expected. Systems leaders therefore have to both embrace complexity and ambiguity and make them understandable and tolerable for others. This entails the ability to 'translate' and interpret what is happening and is reliant on an aptitude for précis and summary on the one hand, together with a skill in the construction and communication of clear explanations and narratives on the other – so condensing the inevitable complexity without oversimplifying it. It also involves 'tuning-out' any background noise in order to isolate and focus on that information which is most salient. All this necessitates endless curiosity and intellectual agility and is hard and demanding work.

Ways of relating (relationships and participation)

Systems leadership is a means of connecting with others which is participatory, collective and based upon what can be achieved through strong and trustworthy relationships, rather than being based upon individual and component contributions. Systems leaders are often working 'beyond the bounds of their authority' (Wheatley, 1999) in situations where they are no longer the 'boss' but have to win consent and legitimacy from stakeholder partners and communities, sometimes in situations that might pose a risk to their reputation or their career. So the attributes that most support this way of working are those of empathy and the ability to adopt the perspective of the other – not just as an end in itself, but as a way to better align vision and goals. It involves acting at all times with transparency, honesty and authenticity and being self-aware.

Meetings are not necessarily the only places where such leadership takes place. The danger of continuing with established ways of working such as conventional meetings, pre-existing agendas, information-sharing and so on is probably something of a blind alley. The ostensible leaders may not be the only, or even the most important, leaders and the real work typically takes place in informal meetings, in one-to-one or small group conversations and in carefully designed workshop settings, rather than in formal settings.

It may not even be possible to obtain complete agreement at the outset, not least because different organisations may have to please their different regulatory bodies and be held to account by different public audiences, so sometimes the means of getting started might be joint action on first steps without full agreement on final goals – the establishment of a 'working path' (Huxham & Vangen, 2005). It means going with 'good enough' approaches and building on them, rather than waiting until the perfect way forward is identified.

Ways of doing (behaviour and actions)

Systems leaders role-model the values which they articulate in every conversation and in every encounter. Such values are embedded in their being, as opposed to something which they just intellectually talk about. They live and breathe them and mirror them in their behaviour.

Through such approaches what is needed are behaviours and action that stimulate, facilitate and enable those actions that are taken by others, both in other parts of the wider system and within their own teams and organisations. It clearly involves making and mending relationships on multiple fronts and winning trust by delivering on promises, giving mutual support and sharing both power and credit. It can include, for example:

- The repurposing and reframing of existing structures and resources in order to address new endeavours.
- Creatively and skilfully using conflict as a means to create energy.
- Balancing risk with opportunity and using the consequences to open up new routes towards a common goal.
- Appropriately de-prioritising personal and organisational interests in pursuit of a common and wider objective. This implies actively ceding power and resources.

If there is simply a continuation of established ways of working (such as consultation and discussion through conventional and formal agenda-based and progress-chasing meetings, the writing of position papers and so on) then:

> If I continue to believe as I have always believed, I will continue to act as I have always acted; and if I continue to act as I have always acted, I will continue to get what I have always got.
>
> *(Ferguson, 1980)*

The requirement is for new and different ways to design and run meetings, using alternative methods drawn from such approaches as, for example, Appreciative Inquiry (Edmonstone, 2006), Future Search (Weisbord & Janoff, 1995) or Conversational Conferences (Pratt et al., 2003). The challenge is to design and run such meetings in different ways, where different perspectives can fruitfully emerge and where the design is of a meeting process which is facilitated, rather than managed. It means creating a space where everyone who joins in feels equally powerful and valued, feels that they can have an equal say and feels respectful of others' views and opinions. It may therefore help to use different labels like 'workshop', 'laboratory' or 'colloquium' for such events in order to signal that it is a space for prototyping new ways of learning and working together.

Good thinking is likely to come from combining the different ways of seeing and perspectives of all the different players. A good starting-point is that everyone there is probably right – everyone can see something that is true, important and worrying for them from their own perspective. It is just that no-one can see it all. It then becomes possible to build something new from the learning that derives from difference.

Ways of being (personal qualities)

These form the 'default operating system' of systems leaders and include the energy, drive and determination, bravery and resilience needed to work together differently, together with the optimism, confidence and willingness required in order to take risks (all of which are qualities attributed to effective leaders in general). Additionally, however, systems leaders display humility, magnanimity, patience and a willingness to be open when things have not gone well.

It means, for example, having shared conversations out loud with other leaders that mirror the conversations which they already have in their own heads, and to do this certainly requires very high levels of trust and integrity. Such conversations need to get under the skin of each partner's hopes, expectations, ways of working, beliefs and experiences. It may mean being courageous and drawing attention to particular problems – the 'elephants in the room' – and not flinching from the difficult conversations that may then ensue.

It also means that systems leaders need to pay attention to their own emotions and to treat themselves well, so that they are, in turn, able to pay attention to the emotional needs of others. Such self-care (Keep, 2013) means asking of themselves such questions as 'What does this make me feel?' and 'How does this affect me?'

These dimensions or ways of systems leadership cannot be treated as alternative 'preferences' or 'character strengths'. It is not possible to concentrate on just one at the expense of another because the alternatives do not seem to be quite so engaging. These are not simply skills, but things which will be happening and have to happen – so attention needs to be paid to all of them. The advantage of systems leadership being a collective activity is that it is across the network of leaders that these dimensions can be attended to, as one person can probably not attend to them all.

Factors that facilitate systems leadership (Hulke et al., 2017)

Certain factors help to facilitate the development of systems leadership. They are:

- *Development of a shared vision and purpose:* This involves shifting from reactive problem-solving towards the gradual building of a positive and compelling vision for the future that explains why the future changed state will be better than the status quo (Bevan et al., 2011). Such a vision needs to be felt by staff at an emotional level – it is not enough for it to be described only in terms of its rationality and logic. It involves systems leaders articulating their deeper aspirations and building collective confidence based upon tangible accomplishments achieved together. Such a shift involves not just creating inspiring visions but also facing difficult truths about the present reality and learning how to use the tension between the vision and the reality as a means to inspire new approaches (Senge et al., 2014). This work takes people beyond pretending that everyone is 'on board' and creating the polite illusion of a cohesive team, towards identifying something which they really want to achieve for service users and for the population concerned. Placing the service user at the heart is key to turning early enthusiasm into practical action. There may be a need to 'go slowly at first to go fast later', so that different groups can develop their understanding of what has brought other partners on board, their perspectives, priorities and pressures. Taking time will be crucial to identifying and resolving differences and developing a shared narrative about what the real shared ambition is. This makes it easier to develop and promote a compelling shared narrative that partners can buy into when it can be seen to lead to tangible benefits for service users and for communities.

- *Ensuring frequent personal contact:* Systems leadership is an activity that cannot be conducted at a distance. It requires a degree of stability from the same individuals and for systems leaders as a 'coalition of the willing' to have regular face-to-face meetings with each other in order to establish the rapport and understanding on which systems leadership hinges and which makes it safe to say risky things. Systems leaders need to address issues as basic as whether they really understand each other sufficiently in order to forge such alliances, as well as whether such mutual trust exists or can be developed. Unless systems leaders understand the worlds that their counterparts are in and the pressures that they are under, they will not be able to frame issues and questions in such a way that gets and holds the attention of their colleagues. It also means aiming to understanding the person behind the role and the different, as well as the shared, motivations and interests that exist among those who are working together.

- *Surfacing and resolving conflicts:* The journey towards systems leadership is rarely straightforward. Agreements will go hand in hand with disagreements, and the latter can be fatal if they are allowed to fester and to undermine relationships and trust. The absence of conflicts though can also be more worrying than their presence, because conflicts occur when difficult truths are confronted, rather than suppressed. Conflicts, challenges and dissent should therefore be welcomed and embraced, rather than resisted, as steps towards building systems leadership, while also recognising that persistent conflicts can be damaging. Surfacing and naming conflict issues is a first step towards working them through and towards creating those conditions in which it feels safe to challenge. It is important to be able to discriminate between those people for whom a very direct conversation (sometimes called 'collaborative thuggery' (Huxham & Vangen, 2005)) is needed and those for whom an idea might have to be planted and allowed to grow.

- *Behaving altruistically towards others:* Leaders who behave altruistically towards each other can play a key role in developing systems leadership (Baumeister & Leary, 1995). It means approaching relationships with peers by asking 'How can I help?' and not 'How can I use our relationship to further my own position and that of my organisation?'. It means not asking 'How can I win in this discussion?', but rather 'How can we succeed together?' As United States President Harry Truman is alleged to have said: 'It's amazing what you can achieve if you don't care who gets the credit.'

- *Committing to working together for the longer-term:* Systems leadership is more likely to happen when leaders know that those with whom they are working are committed to working together for the longer-term. This longevity, continuity and stability is important because of the investment of time and energy needed to build and sustain effective working relationships, and thus to maintain momentum. This investment may only be worth making if there is a reasonable certainty that those with whom they are working are likely to be ongoing partners in transforming the system for which they are mutually responsible.

Additionally, it is important at a very early stage to recognise that time will certainly be needed to enable the individuals and organisations concerned to learn and to adapt to one another and it will therefore be essential to plan and resource a 'budget' (in terms of both time and finance) to invest in the development and sustaining of the capacity to work together (Mervyn & Amoo, 2014).

This chapter has identified who systems leaders are and what they do and has described an 'authorising environment' in which systems leadership can flourish. Six systems leadership personal styles have been highlighted and the factors that facilitate systems leadership noted.

References

Baumeister, R. & Leary, M. (1995) The Need to Belong: Desire for Interpersonal Attachments as a Fundamental Human Motivation, *Psychological Bulletin*, 117(3): 497

Bevan, H., Plsek, P. & Winstanley, L. (2011) *Leading Large Scale Change: A Practical Guide and Postscript*, Coventry: NHS Institute for Improvement and Innovation

Capri, A. (2011) *Quips, Quotes and Quanta: An Anecdotal History of Physics,* London: World Scientific Publishing

Edmonstone, J. (2006) *Building on the Best: An Introduction to Appreciative Inquiry in Health Care*, Chichester: Kingsham Press

Edmonstone, J. (2017) *Action Learning in Health, Social and Community Care: Principles, Practices and Resources*, Abingdon: CRC Press

Ferguson, M. (1980) *The Aquarian Conspiracy: Personal and Social Transformation in our Time*, London: Paladin

Gallos, J. (2008) 'Learning from the Toxic Trenches': The Winding Road to Healthier Organisations and to Healthier Everyday Leaders, *Journal of Management Inquiry*, 17(4): 354–367

Ghate, D., Lewis, J. & Welbourn, D. (2013) *Systems Leadership: Exceptional Leadership for Exceptional Times: Synthesis Paper*, ADCS Virtual Staff College/The Leadership Forum/Colebrook Centre for Evidence & Implementation/Cass Business School, City University, London

Goss, S. (2015) *Systems Leadership: A View from the Bridge*, London: Office for Public Management

Heifetz, R. (1994) *Leadership without Easy Answers*, London: Belknap Press of Harvard University Press

Heifetz, R. & Laurie, D. (1997) The Work of Leadership, *Harvard Business Review*, 75(1): 124–134

Hulke, S., Walsh, N., Powell, M., Ham, C. & Alderwick, H. (2017) *Leading across the Health and Care System: Lessons from Experience*, London: Kings Fund

Huxham, C. & Vangen, S. (2005) *Managing to Collaborate: The Theory and Practice of Collaborative Advantage*, Abingdon: Routledge

Keep, J. (2013) *Developing Self-Care at Work*, PhD thesis, Bristol: University of the West of England

Mervyn, K. & Amoo, N. (2014) *Brief Literature Review on Improvement at Systems Level*, Leeds: Leeds Institute for Quality Healthcare

Pratt, J., Plamping, D. & Gordon, P. (2003) Conversational Conferences: From Ideas to Action, *British Journal of Healthcare Management*, 9(3): 98–103

Revans, R. (2011) *ABC of Action Learning*, Farnham: Gower

Senge, P., Hamilton, H. & Kania, J. (2014) The Dawn of System Leadership, *Stanford Social Innovation Review*, Winter, 27–30

Weisbord, M. & Janoff, S. (1995) *Future Search: An Action Guide to Finding Common Ground in Organisations and Communities*, San Francisco: Berrett-Koehler

Wheatley, M. (1999) *Leadership and the New Science: Discovering Order in a Chaotic World*, San Francisco: Berrett-Koehler

3

DEVELOPING SYSTEMS LEADERSHIP

This chapter considers the kinds of people we might be looking for (and at) for systems leadership. It distinguishes between leadership development and leader development, before exploring the nature of adult learning. It identifies a set of limiting leadership mind-sets (and their antidotes). It examines what is needed in order to learn systems leadership before offering ideas on the appropriate design of learning and development, the need for a learning architecture and the potential 'ingredients' that might form part of the mix.

What kind of people are we looking for (and at)?

There is a continuing debate concerning whether systems leadership can be taught, or whether it simply has to be learned in practice by those with the inherent skills and personality traits needed in order to do it. Those leaders who have been educated and trained in, and who have progressed successfully to, senior positions in their respective employers through demonstrating intra-organisational and even inter-organisational leadership qualities can find ceding their authority and power and making the required shift in mind-set to be very challenging indeed. The very sources of power which they may have relied upon to get them to their current position of authority within their own organisations are unlikely to work in this changed environment. This is because much of the motivation which drives social behaviour is governed by the organising principle of minimising threat and maximising reward. This is embodied in the SCARF model (Rock, 2008) which identifies five domains of human social experience that activate a reward or threat response:

Status (our relative importance to others): Individual leaders (and their organisations) will inevitably experience some level of potential threat to their status with the onset of change.

Certainty (our ability to predict the future): The word 'transformation' is highly threatening to many people, as it disturbs their ongoing certainty.

Autonomy (our source of control over events): The threat to both individual and organisational autonomy has grown over time with increasing centralisation.

Relatedness (our sense of safety with others): A leader's sense of safety is contingent upon trust and mutual relatedness with their peers.

Fairness (our perception of fair exchanges between people): A 'winners and losers' culture is potentially threatening.

Certainly, if those individuals feel the need to take all the credit for achieving change then they are most probably unlikely to make good systems leaders. They would, in any case, not necessarily see what is happening with systems leadership as being any kind of leadership at all, as it has not been mandated in the way that leadership has been in the past, in terms of hierarchical structure and role and of linear ways of working. Such people may not regard systems leadership as even being relevant because they have spent such a long time (and much effort) in climbing up a very different leadership ladder. They may see the business of exploring future system possibilities as merely 'chewing the fat' and as time-wasting talking-shops. One of the biggest challenges for such people is in recognising that it is not possible at the outset to know what to do and that the previous 'fixes' are simply no longer appropriate. For these people there will therefore also be a powerful need to unlearn what they have previously deemed to be accepted normal practice.

This book seeks to capture and embody emerging good practice vis-à-vis systems leadership, but it leans ultimately towards the notion that systems leadership really has to be learned in practice.

Systems leadership is something which ultimately involves everyone within the system (see below). People co-construct their sense of direction through their own unique form of social interaction. Leadership unfolds from the collective encounter in which all those involved play a contributor role, whether they even acknowledge it or not. However, there are some notions of the qualities that both support and enhance systems leadership and these will be present to a lesser or greater degree in everyone concerned, and these can, of course, be further developed. They include:

- *A willingness to align around a shared purpose:* Able to work with others towards a common end and in and for a particular place.
- *Flexibility and agility:* Being able and willing to adapt and change to moveable circumstances.
- *Openness and transparency:* Being visible and accessible to all stakeholders.
- *Able to work reasonably well with uncertainty:* Possessing a high tolerance of ambiguity.

- *Able to build engagement:* Skill in both making and mending working relationships and in really listening to others.
- *A preference for outcomes over managerial processes:* Keeping their 'eyes on the prize' at all times.
- *Balancing co-operation and competition:* Being able to see the advantages and disadvantages of both and to apply them appropriately.
- *Facilitation skills:* In working with others by focusing on interpersonal and inter-group processes, and not just on performance.
- *Creative use of conflict:* Being able to identify, name and address conflicts where they exist and to work with others in order to resolve them.
- *A willingness to think 'beyond the rules':* Not to be hidebound by existing roles, procedures, protocols and by formal guidance, but to be able to see and to explore situations with a set of fresh eyes.
- *Curiosity:* An inquisitive desire to learn and to keep on learning.
- *Valuing of differences:* Seeing different perspectives as opportunities, rather than as problems to be ignored.
- *Disturbing the system:* Encouragement of respectful dissent and a willingness to disrupt existing patterns of thinking and behaviour for the greater good.
- *Tolerating the long game:* Not being bound by short-termism and the need for 'quick wins'.

The journey towards systems leadership may well therefore be difficult, both intellectually and emotionally for some professional and managerial staff, but in the future the environment in which health and social care leaders operate will continue to be characterised by change being the only constant. The complexity, inter-relationships and interdependencies across systems are likely to increase even further. The need to collaborate, integrate and lead in order to secure better outcomes for service users and communities within increasingly constrained resources will inevitably continue. Given this, the need to develop in leaders the ability to operate across systems, of various and changing spatial and organisational dimensions, will become ever more important.

It is also important to remember that leadership development activity works as much through 'generative' causation (that is, by creating those conditions where things can change and move on to destinations as yet unknown) as through 'successionist' causation (or by achieving predictable and pre-known outcomes) (Thorpe et al., 2008).

Leadership development or leader development?

Most leadership development activity to date has unfortunately not been aimed at the intractable or wicked problems which are features of the health and social care system, but rather it has focused on individuals and on their personal knowledge and skills (Jackson & Parry, 2011). This is more accurately described as *leader development*, which reflects the enduring 'allure of heroic leadership' (Bolden et al., 2016). This is a major aspect of the dominant national and international leadership discourse which embodies taken-for-granted assumptions that leadership is an elite practice and a rational endeavour which arises from those characteristics possessed only by a few special and gifted individuals (Rogers, 2007).

For this reason, leadership is seen as emanating from individual leaders, located from the middle to the top of hierarchical organisations (Bolden, 2007). Such an approach is attractive to the holders of such structural positions because it reinforces their sense of being 'special' and also because it appears to offer a sense of continuing hierarchical control. The underlying assumption is that leadership exists only within individuals and that a concentration on individual leaders through the enhancement of their personal attributes, qualities, behaviours, knowledge and skills will develop their 'human capital'. Grounded in psychology, this emphasis embodies what has been called the 'fundamental attribution error' (Ross, 1977) – the tendency to overvalue personality-based explanations of behaviour, while undervaluing situational or contextual explanations. It assumes that leadership can simply be enhanced, for example, by individuals 'knowing themselves better' and there is therefore an inherent belief that the personal development of many individual leaders will lead inexorably to improved organisational learning and thus, in addition to the development of human capital, to the creation of 'social capital', although this may occur as much by accident as design. For example, in a critique of Masters in Business Administration (MBA) programmes Bennis and O'Toole (2004) asserted that while leaders crucially needed to develop judgement (because the facts for rigorous decision-making were rarely available) resolving leadership uncertainties and embracing ethical and social responsibilities played almost no part in the underlying narrative. Analysis was prioritised at the expense of judgement; leadership was reduced to decision-making; decision-making was reduced to analysis and analysis was reduced to a range of different tools and techniques.

There is little or no evidence that the enhancement of individual human capital leads automatically to improved social capital. The investment which has taken place to date into leader and management development in health and social care has probably done wonders for the career progression of those individual leader programme participants, but has largely failed to enhance social capital, defined as the 'goodwill available to individuals and groups. Its source lies in the structure and content of social relations. Its effects flow from the information, influence and solidarity it makes available' (Adler & Kwon, 2002).

One aspect of the focus on individual leader development has been the emphasis on behavioural competences or qualities, currently the most dominant model of leader assessment and development (see Chapter 1). Such an approach seeks to both identify and quantify the skills and abilities required of people in leader roles. Advocates of the competence approach claim that it offers a framework for effective behaviour, objectivity and consistency of approach, evidence-based assessment, a developmental framework and a means of communicating which leader behaviours are perceived as being valuable and desirable. This preference for a competence approach can also be seen as one aspect of the attempt by senior organisational leaders to 'hold things together' in the face of the VUCA/RUPT environments in which 21st century organisations operate and which have led to a blurring of organisational identity and boundaries and given rise to feelings of fragmentation and loss of control (Bolden & Gosling, 2006; Kallinokos, 2003; Child & Rodrigues, 2002).

Unfortunately, competence-based approaches also tend to fragment leadership activity into discrete competences rather than representing it as an integrated whole. They also undermine the importance of the local context, reinforce traditional ways of thinking about leadership and focus on measurable behaviours at the expense of much subtler qualities, such as empathy or trustworthiness. Such approaches assert that *all* leaders (at *all* levels, in *all* professions and in *all* organisations) should aspire to certain competences. While such competences may well be descriptive (especially in relation to those people in 'top' jobs) they are consistently used in a prescriptive way by generalising their applicability to *all* leaders in *all* settings.

The participants in leader development programmes typically report improved confidence and enhanced feelings of self-worth, but this prime focus on individual skills and competences has a number of implications for the development of leadership within any organisation and of the system of which it is a part. It can, for example, serve as socialisation or 'identity regulation' within such organisations (Alvesson & Willmott, 2002). Attempts to shape participants in these programmes via desirable competences and towards 'idealised leader identities' have been critiqued as 'cultural doping' (Raelin, 2008) where participants all come to share a single dominant ideology and values and are therefore unwilling (and seemingly therefore unable) to question such a perspective (Gagnon & Collinson, 2014). Such an approach has also been described as 'training people into submission' (Edmonstone & Havergal, 1995). It has been noted that:

> these opportunities for leadership development are likely to remain highly valued by the chosen, for whom the recognition and self-worth benefits may outweigh the inappropriateness of universal models or the need to resist undesirable shaping. In this way, those chosen for cultural assimilation collude in perpetuating development that ill prepares them to the acknowledged complexity of leadership work.
>
> *(Vince & Pedler, 2018)*

There are a number of possible reasons why this adherence to leader development has become the default position. They are:

- We may well seek to repeat in an adult relationship what we expected from our parents during childhood, in that we prefer the security of someone who is 'in charge' and who is looking out for us (Maccoby, 2004).
- The media-inspired mythology surrounding the 'great man' theory of leadership, a 19th century shibboleth that still exists in many people and cultures (Carlyle, 1849). According to this all events in organisations are controlled by the charisma and intelligence of great men. Apart from the inherent sexism which this embodies, as a result leadership is presented as simply a binary

relationship between the leader and the led. Such a view is amplified consistently by the media, for example in such television programmes as The Apprentice and seems also to be embodied in national and international politics.

- As the dominant ideology in most organisations and societies in the 21st century is that of neoliberalism (Monbiot, 2016), it powerfully serves to cultivate an individualistic mentality of winners (that is, leaders) and losers (the led). This dyadic relationship implies that success and prowess (which are the mark of leaders) are things which are earned through desire, effort and (especially) their innate ability, but the corollary of this is that failure and weakness are also earned and so when individuals (that is, the led) fail to succeed then this is a reflection of inadequate talent or energy on their part (Davies, 2017).
- Those who have succeeded in rising to senior positions in organisational hierarchies are often loath to subsume their power and influence towards a greater good, having succeeded in climbing up their organisation's 'greasy pole'.

The concern is that this leader development simply does not prepare people adequately for the challenges which health and social care systems leadership addresses. It may well encourage individuals to divert their energies into the management of their own careers, for example, through the pursuit of an MBA qualification, and, much more seriously, mislead both the participants in such programmes and their employing organisations into thinking that their salvation lies in just finding the 'right' people with the 'right' qualifications, rather than building the more collaborative efforts required in the complex and uncertain situations of wicked problems.

Most MBA programmes, as mentioned above, essentially develop what Aristotle called 'episteme' or 'knowing that' (the absorbing of information, concepts and models), while systems leadership largely requires what Aristotle called 'techne' or 'knowing how' – pragmatic and context-dependent knowledge grounded in craft and skill (Billsberry & Birnik, 2010). Techne is based upon the assumption that leadership is a 'contact sport, not virtual reality' (Briggs & Briggs, 2009) and is concerned with the 'extraordinisation of the mundane' (Alvesson & Sveningsson, 2003).

Episteme (or knowing that) is largely transmitted via what has been termed a *vicious learning sequence*. Such traditional approaches to learning (as shown in Figure 3.1) seek to provide learners with generic knowledge and skills but then leave the challenge of transferring that learning from the education or training context into the workplace and personal practice of the learners themselves. Learners therefore regularly experience difficulties in applying such learning to their local work settings where there may be few rewards (and possibly even significant disincentives) for trying out something new or different. This is popularly known as the learning transfer problem. As a result, workplace action often gradually tends to 'fizzle out' and come to a full stop.

Techne (or knowing how) can be fostered via a *virtuous learning cycle* (as shown in Figure 3.2). Here learning is focused on seeking improvements for service users and communities, with the result that both the individual learner and their

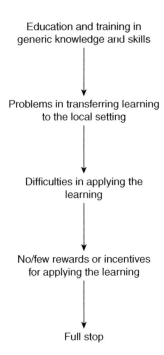

FIGURE 3.1 Vicious learning sequence

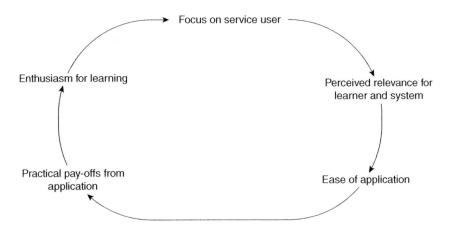

FIGURE 3.2 Virtuous learning cycle

colleagues perceive it as both relevant and easier to apply. As a result, personal and system pay-offs tend to increase their enthusiasm for learning in this way.

If systems leadership embodies an emphasis on collective, rather than individual leadership, then it is largely concerned with the cultivation of what has been termed social capital. The working practices of social capital leaders have been identified (McCallum & O'Connell, 2009) as:

- Not viewing leadership as a rank or a job title, but rather as a position with responsibility for a diverse group of stakeholders.
- Taking a partnership approach and striving to ask good questions of empowered colleagues.
- Working as coaches to staff where the sharing of learning builds collective energy, which in turn leads to the creation and sharing of new understandings.
- Managing the paradox of both collaborating and competing with other agencies and groups.

The differences between leadership development for social capital and leader development for individual human capital are shown in Table 3.1.

TABLE 3.1 The differences between leadership development for social and human capital

Comparison dimension	Development target	
	Individual leader	Leadership
Capital type	Human capital	Social capital
Leadership model	Individual: Personal power Knowledge Trustworthiness	Relational: Commitments Mutual respect Trust
Competence base	Intra-personal	Inter-personal
Skills	Self-awareness: Emotional awareness Self-confidence Accurate self-image	Social awareness: Empathy Service orientation Political awareness
	Self-regulation: Self-control Personal responsibility Adaptability Self-motivation Initiative Commitment Optimism	Social skills: Building bonds Change catalyst Conflict management

Adult learning

Leaders in health and social care are largely mature adults. Adult learning is now properly understood as an organismic or natural 'living' process, rather than as an ego-driven process (Claxton, 1981). This means that it is not something that 'I' do, but something that happens of itself, often in spite of 'I' and not because of it. Learning is also not something which is only confined to formal and structured settings such as educational and training programmes (academic or otherwise), but is also informal in nature (such as through personal and professional networks) – that is, predominantly experiential and non-institutional – and may also be incidental – that is, unintentional and as a by-product of other activity (Marsick & Watkins, 1997). We can therefore say that while individual human beings are naturally 'programmed' to learn, organisations are not.

What is known in adult learning terms is that:

- *Learning starts from not knowing:* It is only when people honestly admit that they do not know how to proceed that they really become open to learning. There can be no experts in those situations in which there are no 'right' answers and no obvious ways to move forward. Where there are no right answers then people must act in order to learn. Learning can thus be seen as a means of sharing and exploring our ignorance.

- *Learning involves the whole person:* People do not usually, in practice, separate their emotions from their intellect. The recent popularity of the concept of Emotional Intelligence is a clear recognition of the critical role that emotion also plays in learning (Goleman, 1996).

- *Much learning is episodic in nature, rather than continuous:* It seems to take place in short bursts of relatively intense activity which absorb the learner's attention and comes to an end when the immediate purpose of such learning has been achieved. People then resort to a much slower pace of learning before the next intensive episode takes place, stimulated by another problem, situation or issue which demands resolution.

- *We feel the urge to learn when we are faced with difficulties we would like to overcome:* Real-world problems provide us with the motivation to learn. People who take responsibility in a situation have the best chance of taking those actions that make a difference. We learn most, and best, when what and how we learn is experienced as being relevant to us.

- *Learning is not just about the assimilation of knowledge, but also about the recognition of what is already known:* Learning is inevitably based upon, and therefore builds on, our previous experience. It involves both what is taught to us and our insights gained from questioning. It is not only the acquisition of yesterday's ideas but also the trying-out of new and unfamiliar ideas. It involves asking useful questions in conditions of uncertainty and therefore involves a degree of risk – the taking of actions that may or may not work.

- *A powerful block to learning is our predisposing way of seeing the world:* Our mind-set or way of seeing the world has inevitably been formed by our previous experience and is made up of our fears, hopes, dreams, speculations, queries, hunches, intuitions, habits, identifications, unconscious projections, half-baked notions, prior training, social conditioning and internalised cultural expectations. These are typically not shared, explicit or even logical when viewed by others but they do contribute to the patterns (of beliefs, traditions, fears, conflicts) that make some things possible and others impossible for each one of us.

- *Revision of mind-sets is easier in a safe and secure atmosphere:* We learn best with and from other people as peers when we are addressing together those pressing difficulties to which no-one knows the solution. Learning is increased when we are asked challenging questions by our peers and reflect on what we did; when we have the time and space to address problems and when we are encouraged, supported and challenged in doing so (Edmonstone, 2011).

Three useful ways of further understanding adult learning are the notions of the ladder of inference, single and double-loop learning and the centrality of reflection.

The ladder of inference

Inferring is largely an automatic and unconscious human learning process (Senge et al., 1994; Argyris, 1985). People operate most of the time using higher-level abstraction in order to process the huge amount of information which they gather through their senses. Thus, assumptions and attributions about other professions and organisations are actually extrapolations from perceived data at various levels of abstraction – a ladder of inference, where the higher the rung on the ladder, the more abstract and less reliable is the inference. This is shown in Figure 3.3.

In the course of any human being's lifetime their mind-sets of attitudes and beliefs become reinforced by their selective attention to events. Attention is most

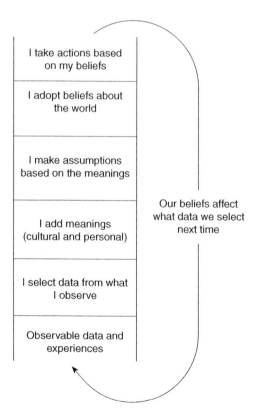

FIGURE 3.3 The ladder of inference

paid to confirming, rather than disconfirming data. Most of the time this is a natural and helpful process, as it helps individuals to avoid information overload and the continuous reappraisal of both people and situations. However, it also means that people operate for most of the time on the basis of their pre-existing biases and prejudices. Thus no two people usually experience the same event in the same way and so their natural mental 'short-cuts' – their assumptions, expectations and biases – can prove to be unhelpful at times.

Problems frequently arise when individuals do not test out their attributions about other people's behaviour. The higher the level of inference, the more difficult it is to be explicit about personal thinking processes and, in those situations perceived as risky or threatening, it often becomes much more difficult. Very often, when things go wrong, the tendency is to attribute to others what are our own weaknesses, by assuming that we all 'fail' for the same reasons. Individuals seek to protect themselves, and the others involved, by not telling them about the negative attributions being made about them – and this is typically considered the 'right' thing to do. Unfortunately, by avoiding confrontation and leaving such attributions untested, they can become self-fulfilling prophecies, even if they are inaccurate.

So, from an individual's experience, certain data are selected to which meanings are added based upon prior personal and cultural experience and these form the basis of the assumptions that are then made and the conclusions that are then drawn. These conclusions enable the individual to adopt beliefs about the world upon which they then base their actions. This is a 'self-sealing' process, as the beliefs adopted then powerfully affect the data selected on the next occasion. Only by breaking this reinforcement, by examining and challenging the assumptions, can deeper learning take place.

Single and double-loop learning (Argyris, 1976; Bateson, 1972; Schon, 1983; Greenwood, 1998)

Single-loop learning is adaptive and tactical learning – simply solving an immediate problem – and so it represents only incremental change. It asks the question 'Are we doing things right?' or 'Are we doing what is specified?' and occurs when goals, values, frameworks and strategies are taken for granted and hence rarely change. It improves the status quo by narrowing the gap between desired and actual positions. It is effectively error detection and correction and the maintenance of a steady state. It is the world of everyday, normal, 'in-the-box' thinking which leaves underlying intentions and processes largely unchallenged and therefore unchanged. Single-loop learning works well for the business of addressing tame problems (see Chapter 1) and is shown in Figure 3.4.

Double-loop learning is where minds and actions are changed as a result of feedback received. Instead of asking 'Are we doing things right?' or 'Are we doing what is specified?', it asks the questions 'Are we doing the right things?' or 'Have we specified the right things to do?' and so calls into question the very nature of the way forward that has been already plotted and the feedback loops that are used to maintain that particular course. These deeper considerations challenge basic assumptions with regard to values, goals, strategies and processes and prompt re-evaluation and reframing – and

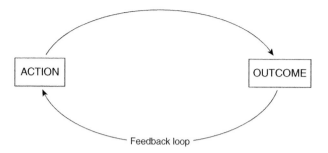

FIGURE 3.4 Single-loop learning

hence more fundamental changes in habits of thinking and acting at both individual and system levels, encouraging people to think and act in new and unfamiliar ways. Double-loop learning (as shown in Figure 3.5) is both less normal and less comfortable as it challenges assumptions, questions what is taken for granted and potentially can stimulate conflict. It represents 'out-of-the-box' thinking and can potentially lead to a redefining of goals, norms, policies, procedures, roles and structures. It is therefore both strategic and generative. Double-loop learning is a necessary means of addressing wicked problems and is therefore essential for systems leadership.

Reflection

Reflection on previous and current actions makes the vital difference between what has been described as having ten years' worth of experience and having one year's worth of experience repeated nine times. Reflection enables a higher level of awareness of the complexities of the internal ('in-here') and the external ('out-

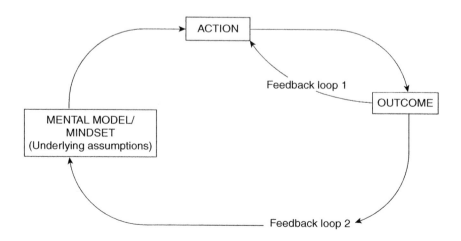

FIGURE 3.5 Double-loop learning

there') worlds and their inter-connectedness. There are five levels of reflection which can enable learning (Hawkins & Shohet, 2012). They are:

- *Noticing things:* Using our senses to hear and feel, without making any judgements or interpretations.
- *Recognising patterns that connect different aspects of things:* This involves 'joining the dots' and seeing the patterns that connect things.
- *Making sense of the patterns:* Only when connecting patterns are recognised is it sensible to seek to understand what is emerging.
- *Shifting the frame of our perception:* This involves a shift away from viewing current experience (which is seen as widely accepted, normal and 'the way things are done round here') and towards a more critical consideration of that experience.
- *Shifting the underlying belief system:* This involves consideration of personal and professional values and motivation – which are often out of conscious awareness.

Systems leadership involves all of these levels but especially the later ones. It has been suggested that: 'Without reflection, we go blindly on our way, creating more unintended consequences, and failing to achieve anything useful' (Wheatley, 2007).

Limiting mind-sets on leadership (and their antidotes)

The leadership field has thus long been dominated by limiting mind-sets. What follows are the conventional assumptions and the emerging alternatives (in italics):

- Leadership is what is done by leaders. *There is no leadership without leaders, followers and a shared endeavour.*
- Leadership resides within people. *Leadership resides in the pattern of relationships and connections between people.*
- Leadership resides at the top. *Leadership is distributed throughout the organisation, wherever responsibility needs to be taken.*
- Leaders are about making change happen in the organisation. *Leaders need to engage with the complex values of stakeholders. Leadership happens at the boundaries.*
- Leaders set the vision and direction for others to follow. *Leadership starts with empathetic listening, then challenging, then orchestrating.*
- Leaders need to get people to understand. *Leaders need to engage hearts, minds and will – in true dialogue.*
- Leadership is about judgement. *Leadership begins when you stop blaming others or making excuses.*
- Leadership is developed by people going on leadership courses. *Leadership development is a mixture of challenging experience and supported reflection.*
- Leaders are the organisational heroes. *True leaders give credit to others and create others as leaders.*
- Leaders have the answers. *The key to leadership lies in the quality of the questions that are asked.*

Therefore, other development approaches are more relevant to the complex and uncertain conditions which systems leadership addresses.

An alternative view

> Instead of starting leadership development with theory and then trying to apply it back into practice, it may be more effective to start with the practical challenges facing an organisation or network and then search for leadership theories and concepts which help the practitioners to make better sense of the complexity of the specific whole system.
>
> *(Bennington & Hartley, 2009)*

Collective approaches to leadership put the emphasis on the involvement and engagement of all those who are located in the situation. This means that leadership learning needs to occur laterally across those connected to each other doing work, as well as vertically. The entire collective has to be engaged in the developmental practices which bring about a new leadership culture (Drath et al., 2008), while 'leaderful practice' (Raelin, 2011) has been described as a relational approach informed by democratic values where: 'Everyone is participating in the leadership of the entity both collectively and concurrently; in other words, not just sequentially, but all together and at the same time' (Raelin, 2018).

Thus leadership (as opposed to leader) development has been identified as:

> expanding the collective capacity of organisational members to engage in leadership roles and processes. Leadership roles refer to those that come with and without formal authority. Leadership processes are those that generally enable groups of people to work together in meaningful ways.
>
> *(Day, 2001)*

It implies constellations of individuals and groups operating in a network and across multiple levels, contributing knowledge, skills, energy and meaning to the task at hand (Atkinson et al., 2015), all acting to make change happen with a clear narrative and a strong personal sense of endeavour. A major element is the capacity of systems leaders to recognise each other, to understand the contribution and value of other systems leaders and to build and sustain a network capable of removing collaboratively the obstacles to change and improvement. By seeing the network as a connected set of people, rather than as a series of organisational structures, it becomes possible to make sense of the different levels, to connect horizontally and vertically, to create the right spaces for the right conversations to be had, and to find ways of resolving difficult and discomforting issues. In this way a critical mass of people can be developed who both believe in systems leadership and also enact it.

It requires people to keep an open mind and to solicit everyone's diverse viewpoints, through constructive dialogue and to accept that learning is not always about the acquisition of new knowledge, but that there will also be a need for both individual managers, professionals and whole organisations forming part of the system to 'unlearn' previously-established beliefs and practices.

The need is to continually work to earn each other's trust and cohesion, while fostering creativity and timeliness. There is also a need to see that any individual's or group's actions are part of a bigger picture that can create a common good. At the level of the individual, people have to be willing to find their voice and to contribute it to the dialogue, while also being open to the inquiry of others. At the interpersonal level people need to relish the exchange of diverse perspectives and out-of-the-box thinking. At the level of the whole system it implies establishing and enacting 'permission' to act within agreed parameters and co-ordinating activity without establishing hierarchical authority.

At the individual, interpersonal and system-wide levels a degree of disturbance is important, since without disturbance it is unlikely that anyone will be willing to challenge assumptions or to change the established ways of doing things. Disturbance is useful, but also difficult to cope with, as the disturbance that makes change possible also serves to make many people anxious, defensive and wary of trusting others – and such anxiety is not conducive to experimentation. The danger is to retreat from more radical ways forward, to do the bare minimum and to argue that the systems leadership route is a worthy one, but mere 'pie in the sky'. Therefore, one aspect of systems leadership involves helping people to manage their anxiety in such a way that enables creative and courageous thinking and action without minimising the scale of the challenge. Acknowledging, and then managing, such fear is an important task. It is also inevitable that there will be 'failures' but it is possible to learn as much by failing as by succeeding and people have to be in place long enough to do the learning. As the playwright Samuel Beckett said 'Ever tried. Ever failed. No matter. Try again. Fail again. Fail better.'

Such leadership development accepts that leadership exists in a context which is essentially chaotic and uncertain and seeks to develop what the poet John Keats called 'negative capability' (Keats, 1899), which enables working creatively with complexity and the anxiety which it provokes. It involves an acceptance that not everything can be resolved and a receptive intuition in the face of what is not known. It assumes the concept of 'emergence' – a letting-go of the sense that there is always an answer and that someone else is always in control. Instead, there is an acceptance that there are no 'right' answers out there – only good ideas and possibilities. It assumes that very little can be predicted in advance and involves a balancing of tensions between freedom and order and between action and reflection (Kenny, 1999).

What is needed to learn systems leadership?

People need more real-time learning from progress, challenge and setbacks: Online case studies, large conferences, national 'how to' guidance based upon 'best practice' and 'roll-outs' of the same are typically about showcasing success stories and promoting particular places, programmes or individuals. People are less likely to transfer 'best practice' from outside their context and are more likely to improvise; creating structures and processes that work for them, using a pragmatic evidence-based approach, rather than a magical 'one-best-way' (Memon & Kinder, 2015). Case studies, conferences, guidance and rollouts do not provide the space in which to have frank discussions about what did not work (as well as what did), including the pitfalls, mistakes and difficulties faced along the way. It is not always possible to simply replicate an initiative from elsewhere because local teams also need to consider how their immediate context (such as history, the availability of resources, the culture and the staff mix) may affect implementation and then adapt their approach accordingly. These are aspects which are rarely captured in the polished version of a case study or talk, which are often more about promoting an individual or organisation, rather than embodying honest reflection and evaluation. As a result, many people are highly sceptical of 'best practice' examples, which are often presented as a 'success' by those involved, without any kind of independent evaluation to support this assertion. For the complex challenges which systems leadership involves there is unlikely to be any single and straightforward solution that can be adopted off the shelf. A successful approach in one setting does not automatically translate into similar results elsewhere, but this 'one-size-fits-all' approach has become something of a sacred cow. Often, instead, the approaches needed are context-specific and 'best practice' examples rarely set out the specific elements of the wider environment that contributed to success, so providing limited insight into whether an approach is likely to work well in another place. Context is a critical component of success. What people really need to learn is 'best fit', rather than 'best practice' – those activities that can be implemented flexibly and adapted to suit local circumstances.

People need opportunities to 'dig deeper' into the messy reality of implementation: General and descriptive examples that over-focus on the merits of a single approach, such as, for example, co-located teams, without any further insights into how this was achieved in practice and the journey taken to get there, simply do not go far enough. They fail to take into account the differing starting points and circumstances which can make the information available and the associated general principles unworkable in the specific context and politics of another local place. What is needed instead includes detail on where an initiative came from, how it developed and the ways of working that might be applicable elsewhere. People will then need the time and ability to reflect, plan and experiment, rather than simply comply with someone else's blueprint.

The best way to do this is through face-to-face conversations that allow people to break out of professional and organisational silos: Connecting people virtually or uploading case studies online simply does not provide the necessary opportunities to get deeper into the detail of a programme or activity, to reflect on what is and is not working well and to build the relationships that are needed to make systems leadership a reality. People need opportunities to ask questions and to dig deeper into what can and cannot be applied in a particular context. Such conversations need to be purposeful and to help people tackle real issues or they risk being turned into a talking-shop or a distraction.

Local and peer-led approaches ensure the necessary trust and credibility to make learning relevant to local priorities: National initiatives, no matter how well-intentioned, are often perceived as a form of performance management in disguise, and so prevent honest and purposeful conversations from taking place. A legitimate, credible and neutral 'convenor' or facilitator may be essential to ensure that honest conversations take place, given the cultural differences that may block effective working and learning (Wilson et al., 2016).

Designing learning and development for systems leadership

There are a series of maxims which can act as design principles in considering the development of systems leadership (Walmsley & Miller, 2008; Anderson et al., 2009, Wilkinson, 2009; Malby, 2007). They are:

- *Real change takes place in real work, in real time, with real people:* This means that development activity needs to be always co-designed involving both the organisations concerned (and reflecting their efforts and priorities) and the people who are undertaking their current and anticipated future work. 'Real work' is the actual work that the stakeholder organisations and the people within them are engaged on. The people who do the work do the change and people own what they create.
- *Start with 'what is':* There has to be an understanding amongst people taking part in any development activity about the shared reality of the current situation. Such a shared reality comes from exploring current behaviours – with how work is currently done. Telling stories about lived experiences, for example, can serve to uncover current patterns of behaviour. The 'what is' picture needs to be one that is shared across the partner stakeholders. It is really important to start with 'what is' – with an agreed notion of the present situation shared between all the major stakeholders. This means that there has to be an understanding within the system and among the people taking part in the developmental activity about what is going on here and now. The starting-point needs to be embedded in current behaviours – how we go about our work, not in espoused beliefs about how we go about our work.
- *Start anywhere, but follow it everywhere:* From this work can then extend in many directions. Change can be initiated everywhere, as parts of the system can go 'cold' if change is too staged and sequential. People who were excited at an early stage may begin to feel that their part of the system is not changing and that attention has moved elsewhere – so the danger is that they may drop out or lose interest.
- *Begin with the end in mind:* Explicitly focus on improvements for service users and communities and what can be learned from them.
- *Address system-wide issues:* Sharing and comparing across professions and organisations helps to understand and work across the whole system.

- *Be explicit about underlying values:* The values underlying any programme or development activity need to be both clear and shared. Participants in such programmes would then be encouraged to reflect upon their own value-set and their 'theory-in-use' through a process of critical reflection.
- *Embrace diversity:* Recognise that learning comes from understanding and appreciating difference. This means including processes that enable participants to learn and understand other people's roles and work – their ways of working and ways of understanding. Make time for participants to 'step into each other's shoes'.
- *Don't just talk about it – do it:* Talking about work is not the same as doing work. There have to be changes in behaviour and practical action. This is expressed well as follows:

A man may well learn to talk about taking action simply by talking about taking action (as in classes at a business school) but to learn to take action (as something distinct from learning to talk about action) then he needs to take action (rather than talking about taking action) and to see the effect, not of talking about taking action (at which he may appear competent), but of taking the action itself (at which he may fall somewhat short of competent).

(Revans, 1971)

- *Amplify what works:* Appreciative Inquiry (see below) highlights that some things already work well to a degree. This means that there is a need to uncover and make much more of such assets. Work with examples of promising practices to increase understanding of how to initiate, generate, sustain, develop and learn from new practices that support the direction of travel.
- *Keep connecting the system to more of itself:* Regular review, evaluation and feedback is necessary. Include processes to review the impact of changed behaviours. Develop feedback loops which powerfully influence performance and reward systems. Be open to ideas from outside. Ensure that changes go 'viral'.
- *Address sustainability:* Actively consider how the gains achieved in personal and system improvement and effectiveness can endure and extend beyond the duration of a single programme or development activity.

This means that rather than locating leadership development away from the workplace, it needs to take place in or close to the very settings where the work is being performed. Through conversation and reflection and on a just-in-time basis, participants can focus on the challenges which they face, the dilemmas with which they are dealing and the processes that they are using. Thus the workplace comes to be viewed as a perfectly acceptable place in which to learn about leadership. Leadership itself can then be seen as 'self-correcting' as people engage and learn with and from one another, reflect on their own actions and consequently learn to reconstruct their practices. It not only advances new skills and attitudes but also opens up space for innovative ways to accomplish work or even to re-conceive how work might be done in the first place.

A learning architecture

Therefore, while there may be a mix of developmental activities intended to foster systems leadership, it will be important to ensure that these are mutually supportive and not experienced as a set of disparate 'initiatives'. What is required is a learning architecture – the way the system 'promotes and structures learning, both individual and organisational' (Wilhelm, 2005), in other words, a means of capturing and sharing emergent learning and feeding it back into the system. It involves a system-wide, systematic and co-ordinated effort at learning and sharing across the entire system which draws upon more specific activities which historically have always been experienced as more tactical in nature and aimed only at specific challenges or at particular groups of staff. The aim is to enhance 'systemic eloquence' – the ability of parts of a system to talk well to each other (Edmonstone, 2017). The notion of a learning architecture is important because:

- The promotion and facilitation of both individual and system learning requires its own strategy and structure, ranging from senior champions to local infrastructure.
- Without a systematic approach to developing and harnessing the learning of people in different parts of the system, learning will be limited to isolated pockets or cultural islands and will be blocked by numerous barriers and boundaries to transmission and exchange.
- Within the field of cybernetics the Law of Requisite Variety (Ashby, 1958) proposes that for any system to adapt to its external environment, its internal controls and means of adaptation must incorporate the variety found in that environment. If the internal variety is reduced, then the system will be unable to cope with the external variety. So internal variety should be welcomed and exploited as a vital means of fostering innovation and learning.

There can be no standard 'one-size-fits-all' blueprint for the design of such a system learning architecture because it will need to reflect the specific circumstances and nature of the particular system concerned, the context or setting within which it operates and the key stakeholders who are involved. What is clear, however, is that the design of such a learning architecture ultimately implies major changes to pre-existing education and training arrangements, performance management and the reward and recognition policies within the existing organisations which are part of the system (Pedler et al., 2007). As the nature of such a learning architecture will be both collaborative and collective, the processes by which it is designed and created should also be collaborative and collective – that is, it should involve all the significant stakeholders/partners. Unless there is such a collaborative effort, it is unlikely that the learning architecture design created will have the ownership and 'buy-in' which will be essential for success. There is a danger that organisational power and politics may serve to constrain as well as enhance such effort and the design process will need to recognise this and plan to deal with it (Lawrence et al., 2005). There therefore needs to be a clear realisation that learning for systems leadership is actually a 'core business' of the health and social care system.

Learning 'ingredients'

If it is accepted that most existing leadership development is flawed because it simply concentrates on putting more knowledge into a leader's mind through stand-alone programmes designed to introduce new models, tools and techniques, then systems leaders need to undergo a more in-depth and complex development journey in order to expand their leadership capability, develop their minds to a higher cognitive level and enable them to adapt and think in a more complex, systemic, strategic and interdependent fashion. Their habitual routines and thinking styles need to be (re)tested, refined and solidified, with three primary conditions – 'heat experiences', 'colliding perspectives' and 'elevated sense-making' interwoven in a longitudinal balanced process (Petrie, 2014; 2015):

Heat experiences: These are opportunities that disrupt a leader's habitual thinking patterns and can be purposed to stretch a leader beyond their comfort zone and into new and more advanced modes of thinking. Examples might include leading a difficult meeting, taking on a challenging or new project or working with a very diverse multi-professional team.

Colliding perspectives: These are situations that expose people to others with quite different views, backgrounds and thinking to their own and enable them to listen actively to others' views and opinions; to be challenged, to take on board ideas that differ from their own and to be willing to adapt and change.

Elevated sense-making: This involves time for reflection, coaching, mentoring and professional conversations. It addresses the challenge of 'so what?' and requires the leader to make meaning and sense of their role and activity within the wider system.

The ingredients which enable these conditions can co-exist and support each other within such an overall learning architecture and might well involve some combination of the following:

- *Action learning:* Action learning is:

   a method of both individual and organisational development based upon small groups of colleagues meeting over time to tackle real problems or issues in order to get things done – reflecting and learning with and from their experience and from each other as they attempt to change things.

   (Edmonstone, 2017)

Small groups of around eight people come together on a regular basis and work to a set of jointly-agreed ground-rules. They work together on work-based issues, problems or questions which members of the group or 'set' bring. Through careful and active listening and useful questioning they support and challenge each other in addressing the challenges which they face. Action takes place back in the workplace and is reported on and discussed at the next set meeting in an iterative manner. The set typically works with a facilitator who is especially active in the early phase, but sets may mature and move on to become self-facilitated. Multi-agency or system-wide sets offer a useful and powerful development means of enhancing systems leadership.

Appreciative Inquiry: The traditional approach to problem-solving, which is characteristic of working on Tame problems, operates as follows:

- A problem is identified.
- The problem is defined and analysed.
- Solutions to the problem are analysed and prioritised.
- Action planning takes place – goals and targets are set.
- Action takes place.

There are negative side-effects to this approach, because:

- It focuses on what isn't working, rather than what is.
- It focuses on failures and amplifies them.
- The only time that people pay attention to learning is when they have apparently 'failed'.
- The approach therefore encourages 'languages of deficit'.

Appreciative Inquiry (Cooperrider & Whitney, 1999) starts from a different set of assumptions, which are that:

- In every group, organisation or system, something works.
- What we focus on becomes our reality and we filter out much of the rest.
- Reality is created in the moment – and there are multiple realities.
- Asking questions influences individuals and groups in some way.
- People have more confidence and comfort on a journey to an unknown future when they take with them parts of the known past.
- What we carry forward should be the best bits of the past.
- It is important to value differences.
- The language that we use creates our reality.

So the principles underlying Appreciative Inquiry are:

- Appreciate the best of what exists and people's hopes for the future.
- Apply knowledge of what works and what is possible.
- Provoke the imagination regarding new ways of organising creative improvements.
- Collaborate through collective capacity – building and sharing expertise and resources.

Appreciative Inquiry operates to the model of:

- *Discover* the best of what is good now through stakeholder engagement and exploration of the 'best' experiences and hopes for the future.

- *Dream* – envision what might be possible. Develop provocative propositions and establish principles. Create a picture of an ideal future based on the very best of the present.
- *Design* what the ideal should be. Address the practical implications and develop strategies, structures and resources.
- *Deliver* – innovate what should be. Ensure achievement and then sustain, learn and adjust.

Appreciative Inquiry ensures that a degree of continuity of existing good practice is built into emerging future developments and serves to act as an 'insurance' against any cynicism regarding new 'initiatives'.

Attachments: This involves an individual moving from their current role for an agreed period of time and being 'attached' to another systems leader in the same or another agency. Typically, they act as an assistant or helper to that person, undertaking tasks under the overall supervision of the systems leader. Being attached in this way gives the 'attachee' exposure to different and more varied challenges than might exist within their role, as well as the experience of working with a more senior person dealing with more strategic, rather than operational issues. For this reason, attachments are very suited to junior or budding systems leaders. Careful management of the exit from the 'parent' organisation and entry into the 'host' agency is essential and requires brokerage through a 'dating agency' function at the outset, together with support to the individual 'attachee' at all stages.

Awaydays: These are days on which a group of staff (a team, a project group) meet at a venue away from the workplace and all its pressures in order to review their progress to date, discuss emergent issues and plan future actions. There is often an internal or external facilitator working with the group to support the process. Awaydays can serve to accelerate decision-making and help to build and enhance working relationships. They can also be used for teambuilding activities.

Buddy pairs: This is a procedure in which two people work closely together so that they are able to monitor and help each other. It often involves more experienced individuals being paired with less experienced ones, but the possibilities extend beyond this. It can encourage open and effective dialogue between peers and help to create a collaborative learning environment in which peers are less hesitant to raise questions. It is particularly relevant as a means of protecting young systems leaders by buddying them with more experienced individuals.

Coaching: Coaching (which is the most common development method used worldwide for leadership development) (Garvey et al., 2009) is an active partnership built on trust and respect, where both the coach and the coachee attend carefully to each other. There has to be some agreed purpose for coaching, often focused on achieving personal and/or system goals. It is not generally assumed that the coach needs to have any direct experience of the coachee's role. There are also agreed boundaries, both in the practice of coaching and in what is covered by coaching – it is not the same, for example, as psychotherapy, mentoring or counselling and all coaching sessions are clear of any hidden agendas or manoeuvring. For coaching to be effective the *coachee*:

- Has to be committed to the coaching relationship in terms of both time and energy.
- Has to be willing to disclose personal experiences and feelings honestly.
- Needs to be willing to explore their values and beliefs.
- Needs to be open to feedback from the coach.
- Enjoys exploring possible actions and their consequences with the coach.

While the *coach* will:

- Be committed to the coaching relationship.
- Understand their own values, beliefs and motives.
- Be able to play different roles – as variously a sounding-board, challenger, conscience, professional friend, and 'safe container'.
- Have well-developed skills of active listening, questioning, clarifying, summarising and reflecting.
- Be willing to confront the coachee's issues.

Coaching usually has a set duration – an agreed number of coaching 'sessions' and is structured with meetings scheduled in advance on a regular basis.

Conversational conferences: These are designed to engage participants' practical experience and interaction with those of external experts; to promote conversations and networking that works and to promote implementation after the event. This is pursued through focus on a shared task; topicality; opportunities for mutual support and networking; updating and opportunities for question-and-answer and sharing practice (Pratt et al., 2003).

Future Search: This is a structured large group approach which has the primary purpose of system-wide strategic planning and is particularly applicable when enabling diverse, and possibly conflicting, groups to find common ground for constructive action and new approaches to address wicked problems. A couple of days are necessary, with a long lead-time and preparation through a steering group made up of representatives of the various stakeholders. Part of the purpose is to get representatives of the whole system in the same room and working together (Weisbord & Janoff, 1995).

Open Space: This is a self-organising practice that enables all kinds of people to work on what matters to them. The outcome is unknowable. The practice is a key set of organising principles. It requires no facilitation at all beyond setting up the process and the dialogue at the end. It invites people in a system to take responsibility for issues they care about with others who also have energy for that issue. Participants create their own agenda, running discussion groups and action planning around the things that matter to them, in relation to a key organising complex question. The four governing principles for Open Space are – whoever comes are the right people;

whatever happens is the only thing that could have; whenever it starts is the right time, and when it's over, it's over (Owen, 1997).

Mentoring: Mentoring is 'off-line (i.e. non-hierarchical) help from one person to another to assist them with addressing significant career and life transitions by creating reflective space' (Clutterbuck, 2001). It is a process for the informal transmission of knowledge, social capital and psychosocial support which is perceived by an individual to be relevant to their work or professional development. It entails informal communication, usually face-to-face and over a sustained period of time, between a person who is understood to have greater relevant knowledge, wisdom or experience (the mentor) and a person understood to have less (the mentee). The mentor helps to guide the mentee through a long-term relationship of learning, dialogue and challenge. The focus is on the mentee as a person and not on targets or performance. Mentoring can be both informal and formal in nature. In the case of the former, it usually involves the mentee approaching someone to act as a personal mentor, based upon that person's credibility. The latter is a more structured process supported organisationally and involves the matching of both mentor and mentee through some form of 'dating agency' (Connor & Pokora, 2007).

Organisational raids: This is a group learning opportunity where staff from one organisation in a system visit another to learn how they manage a particular issue or range of issues, exploring the organisation's philosophical and policy approaches and developing some insight into working practices. Both parties concentrate on transferring learning from the event (which typically lasts a day), as the aim is one of widening horizons and developing insight in both directions. In local government in England this approach is called 'peer challenge' (Local Government Association, 2016).

Schwartz rounds: This is a structured forum where staff come together regularly to discuss the emotional and social aspects of working. The purpose is to understand the challenges and rewards that are intrinsic to providing care – but the emphasis is not on problem-solving. Schwartz rounds can help staff feel more supported in their job, allowing them protected time and space to reflect on their role. As a result, they feel less stressed and isolated and have increased insight and appreciation of each other's roles. They also help to reduce hierarchies between staff and to focus attention on the relational aspects of care.

Secondments: This takes an individual out of his or her normal workplace and places them in a different working environment for a defined period of time, usually in a different agency, thus encouraging cross-fertilisation. Sometimes this takes the form of a job swap between two individuals who then both have an opportunity to try out a different role but can meet each other for consultation and advice. Secondments can foster inter-agency learning and may require a 'dating agency' function to facilitate agreement between the individuals and the agencies concerned. The success of a secondment depends upon careful management of the exit process from the 'parent' organisation and entry into the 'host' organisation, as the expectations of all parties need to be clear at the outset. Similarly, the re-entry of the 'secondee' into their parent agency needs to be handled in a sensitive manner. As with attachments, secondments require careful support at all stages.

Shadowing: Shadowing peers in other parts of the system can help to develop insights into how others work and to build relationships. Careful choice of who to shadow and what the learning intentions are form vital preparation. Issues of potential confidentiality might also need to be agreed beforehand. After the event reflection on what has been learned and what can be applied is crucial.

Speakers: Speakers from other agencies can be invited to speak to groups of employees, describing the roles they fulfil and the challenges which they face, followed by questions and answers. Careful briefing of visiting speakers and skilful facilitation of such sessions are necessary. This gives staff insights into the world of people working in other parts of the system.

Team development: There is a plethora of teams within health and social care organisations, some formed from a single profession, but increasingly multi-professional and multi-agency. However, many of these are extremely large groupings for which the term 'team' is something of a misnomer and these have even been branded as 'pseudo-teams' and are probably more realistically described as networks. Research suggests that, ideally, teams should not exceed 8 to 12 people (West, 2012) because increases in team membership beyond this size mean that team members become less clear about the team purpose and objectives, find information sharing much more difficult, interact with each other less and feel that they have less influence over decision-making. They also perceive that there is less support for their ideas for new and improved ways of doing things. Larger teams experience greater strains on effective communication because the number of communication channels increases with the addition of each new team member until it becomes difficult for team members to share important information effectively. One way around this is to have detailed protocols for how the team should work together so that mutual understanding and human closeness is less critical. Even so, the creation of fixed rules and processes for how to work together cannot entirely prevent misunderstandings, especially in crisis situations or when unanticipated problems arise.

Nevertheless, there is a growing recognition that inter-agency and inter-professional teams are critical to successful change, that teamwork is certainly an essential aspect of systems leadership and so the exploitation of the diversity within teams is increasingly seen as valuable (West & Lyubovnikova, 2013). It has recently been suggested that: 'Leaders must keep sight of the importance of teamwork, flexibility, agility and broad vision in local optimisation and to prevent siloes' (Holbeche, 2018).

Using the interesting analogy of a jazz band, it has been proposed that: 'Leadership has to be fluid, allowing specific people to lead when they have the key skills and then step away from leadership to make room for other contributions. Leading and supporting take turns and both matter' (Pendleton, 2018).

Research has revealed that for multidisciplinary teams in health and social care to work successfully there are a set of enablers that should be in place (Miller, 2018):

- *Clear purpose:* Such teams need a defined role that requires team members to interact across professional and disciplinary boundaries.
- *Organisational support:* The organisations which employ the staff and the partnership bodies overseeing this area of work must provide support. This should include public endorsement (and thus legitimacy), ensuring that the team has the necessary resources, and developing integrated performance systems.
- *Team leadership:* Team leaders should be facilitative in their approach and encourage different contributions from team members, but also be directional when necessary. Awareness of team dynamics and a willingness to challenge poor collaborative practice are important qualities of such a team leader.
- *Collaborative opportunities:* Teams must have physical space and time for their members to engage across professions and disciplines. This enables them to improve communications and better understand each other's roles and resources.
- *Person-centric:* There is a danger that teams can become too inwardly-focused on their own functioning. This can lead to service users, carers and families feeling more, rather than less, excluded from discussions about their care.
- *Role diversity:* There is no magic formula for such teams. Rather the mix of professions and practitioners must respond to the needs of the population concerned while being small enough to allow team members to know each other.
- *Evidence-focused:* Teams require timely and accurate evidence of their shared impact. Structured opportunities for teams to reflect on this evidence are among the more impactful means to strengthen their work.

The ultimate vision for integrated multidisciplinary teams would be one that involved self-organising with devolved authority and clear accountability to a 'host' organisation. Different professions and individuals would take the lead at different times depending upon the particular issue or circumstance.

Improving team performance can therefore be achieved by (Page, 2007):

- Making sure that team members have plenty opportunities to interact with each other.
- Ensuring that multiple ways of looking at issues are welcomed.
- Consulting dissenters – those people who may think differently.
- Involving as many people as possible who have relevant information.
- Balancing diversity with ability.
- Not stereotyping.
- Maintaining humility in the face of challenges.

The differences between more traditional leadership and collective team-based leadership are shown in Table 3.2.

Teamwork development can often take place during Awaydays. On such occasions, the emphasis is on the team clarifying such matters as the team's:

- *Goals:* What is the purpose of the team? What does it exist for?
- *Roles:* These could include both the number and nature of formal roles such as Chair, Convenor and Note-taker, but also could consider the appropriate balance of team roles (Belbin, 2010).
- *Procedures:* What are the means by which decisions are made within the team? Is the team only consultative and the team leader ultimately decides? Is a consensus of views to be sought? Does majority voting have a part to play?
- *Process:* What is the nature of interpersonal relationships within the team? How positive and supportive are team members for each other? How is conflict in the team dealt with?

World Café: World café is a structured conversational process for knowledge-sharing in which groups of people discuss a topic at several tables, with individuals switching tables periodically and getting introduced to the previous discussion at their new table by a 'table host'. A café ambience is created in order to facilitate conversation. As well as speaking and listening, participants can be encouraged to write on flipcharts on the table, so that when people change tables, they can see what previous members have written as well as hearing the table host's view of what has been happening. Although pre-defined questions are agreed at the beginning, outcomes are not decided in advance. The underlying assumption is that collective discussion can shift people's conceptions and encourage collective action (Brown & Isaacs, 2005).

TABLE 3.2 Traditional leadership development and collective team-based leadership compared

	Traditional leadership	*Collective team-based leadership*
Responsibility for team performance	Leader	Team supported by leader
Control over decisions	Leader	Team involvement
Leader position power	Emphasised	De-emphasised
Leader interactions	With individuals	Collectively and with individuals
Team process maintenance	Little focus on this	Emphasised and shared
Socio-emotional processes	Ignored	Observed and managed
Expressing needs and feelings	Discouraged	Encouraged

The underlying cultural values which underpin the development of such a system learning architecture are (Davies & Nutley, 2004):

- *Celebration of success:* If excellence is to be pursued with vigour and commitment, its attainment must be valued right across the system culture.
- *Absence of complacency:* The old adage 'If it ain't broke, don't fix it' simply does not apply. Instead, innovation and change are valued across the system and this also involves identifying current good practice and ensuring that it is carried forward.
- *Tolerance of mistakes:* Learning from failure is a prerequisite for development and this means accepting the positive spin-offs from errors, rather than seeking to blame and to scapegoat. It does not, however, imply tolerance of routinely poor performance from which no lessons are learned.
- *Belief in human potential:* People are valued for their creativity, energy and innovation, so their personal and professional development is both cherished and fostered.
- *Recognition of tacit knowledge:* Those individuals closest to the action have the best and most intimate knowledge concerning both potential and flaws. So their tacit knowledge is valued and there is a systematic enlargement of their discretion, responsibility and capability.
- *Openness:* The sharing of knowledge emphasises informal channels and personal contacts over any written reporting procedures. So cross-professional and cross-agency teams, rotation of staff and the other 'ingredients' identified above are all essential components.
- *Trust:* For individuals to give of their best, to take appropriate risks and to develop their capacity, they must trust that such activities will be appreciated and valued. In particular, they must be confident that should they err then they will be supported and not castigated. Without such trust, learning is a faltering process.

This chapter has considered the kind of people systems leaders are and has examined the distinction between leader development and leadership development, noting that systems leadership is best developed by the latter. It has explored adult learning, with particular reference to the ladder of inference, single and double-loop learning and reflection. Limiting mind sets on leadership have been identified, together with their antidotes. An alternative approach to developing systems leaders has been outlined and design principles described as a means of constructing a systems leadership learning architecture. Finally, some of the potential 'ingredients' of such a learning architecture have been noted and the underpinning cultural values have been highlighted.

References

Adler, P. & Kwon, S. (2002) Social Capital: Prospects for a New Concept, *Academy of Management Review*, 27(2): 17–40

Alvesson, M. & Sveningsson, S. (2003) Managers Doing Leadership: The Extraordinisation of the Mundane, *Human Relations*, 56(12): 1435–1459

Alvesson, M. & Willmott, H. (2002) Identity Regulation as Organisational Control, *Journal of Management Studies*, 39(5): 619–644

Anderson, L., Malby, B., Mervyn, K. & Thorpe, R. (2009) *The Health Foundation: Position Statement on Effective Leadership Interventions*, Leeds: Centre for Innovation in Health Management, University of Leeds

Argyris, C. (1976) *Increasing Leadership Effectiveness*, New York, NY: Wiley

Argyris, C. (1985) *Strategy, Change and Defensive Routines*, Boston, MA: Pitman Publishing

Ashby, W. (1958) Requisite Variety and its Implications for the Control of Complex Systems, *Cybernetica* 1(2): 83–99

Atkinson, J., Loftus, E. & Jarvis, J. (2015) *The Art of Change Making*, London: Leadership Centre

Bateson, G. (1972) *Steps to an Ecology of Mind*, Chicago, IL: University of Chicago Press

Belbin, M. (2010) *Team Roles at Work*, 2nd edition, Abingdon: Routledge

Bennington, J. & Hartley, J. (2009) *'Whole Systems Go': Improving Leadership across the Whole Public Service System*, Sunningdale: National School of Government

Bennis, W. & O'Toole, J. (2004) How Business Schools Lost Their Way, *Harvard Business Review* (May): 1–9

Billsberry, J. & Birnik, A. (2010) Management as a Contextual Practice: The Need to Blend Science, Skills and Practical Wisdom, *Organisation Management Journal*, 7(2): 171–178

Bolden, R. & Gosling, J. (2006) Leadership Competencies: Time to Change the Tune?, *Leadership*, 2(2): 147–163

Bolden, R. (2007) *A Yearning for the Vast and Endless Sea: From Competence to Purpose in Leadership Development*, Exeter: Centre for Leadership Studies, University of Exeter

Bolden, R., Witzel, M. & Linacre, N. (Eds.) (2016) *Leadership Paradoxes: Rethinking Leadership for an Uncertain World*, Abingdon: Routledge

Briggs, M. & Briggs, I. (2009) *Developing Your Leadership in the Early Years*, London: Continuum

Brown, J. & Isaacs, D. (2005) *The World Café: Shaping our Futures through Conversation*, San Francisco: Berrett-Koehler

Carlyle, T. (1849) *On Heroes, Hero Worship, and the Heroic in History*, Boston: Houghton-Mifflin

Child, J. & Rodrigues, S. (2002) Corporate Governance and New Organisational Forms: The Problem of Double and Multiple Agency, Paper presented at Joint Symposium on Renewing Governance and Organisations: New Paradigms of Governance?, Denver, CO, Academy of Management

Claxton, G. (1981) *Wholly Human: Western and Eastern Visions of the Self and its Perfection*: London: Routledge & Kegan Paul

Clutterbuck, D. (2001) *Everyone Needs a Mentor: Fostering Talent at Work*, 3rd edition, London: Chartered Institute of Personnel & Development

Connor, M. & Pokora, J. (2007) *Coaching and Mentoring at Work: Developing Effective Practice*, Maidenhead: McGraw-Hill/Open University Press

Cooperrider, D. & Whitney, D. (1999) *Appreciative Inquiry*, San Francisco: Berrett-Koehler

Davies, H. & Nutley, S. (2004) Organisations as Learning Systems, in Kernick, D. (Ed.) *Complexity and Healthcare Organisation: A View from the Street*, Abingdon: Radcliffe Medical Press

Davies, W. (2017) *The Limits of Neoliberalism: Authority, Sovereignty and the Logic of Competition*, London: Sage Publications

Day, D. (2001) Leadership Development: A Review in Context, *Leadership Quarterly*, 11: 581–613

Drath, W., McCauley, C., Palus, C., Van Velsor, E., O'Connor, P. & McGuire, J. (2008) Direction, Alignment, Commitment: Toward a More Integrative Ontology of Leadership, *The Leadership Quarterly*, 19(6): 635–653

Edmonstone, J. & Havergal, M. (1995) The Death (and Rebirth?) of Organisation Development, *Health Manpower Management*, 21(1): 28–33

Edmonstone, J. (2011) *Action Learning in Healthcare: A Practical Handbook*, London: Radcliffe Publishing

Edmonstone, J. (2017) *Action Learning in Health, Social and Community Care: Principles, Practices and Resources*, Abingdon: CRC Press

Gagnon, S. & Collinson, D. (2014) Rethinking Global Leadership Development Programmes: The Inter-Related Significance of Power, Context and Identity, *Organisation Studies*, 35(5): 645–670

Garvey, R., Stokes, P. & Megginson, D. (2009) *Coaching and Mentoring: Theory and Practice*, London: Sage

Goleman, D. (1996) *Emotional Intelligence: Why It Can Matter More Than IQ*, New York: Bantam Books

Greenwood, J. (1998) The Role of Reflection in Single- and Double-Loop Learning, *Journal of Advanced Nursing*, 27(5): 1048–1053

Hawkins, P. & Shohet, R. (2012) *Supervision in the Helping Professions*, 4th edition, Maidenhead: Open University Press

Holbeche, L. (2018) *The Agile Organisation: How to Build an Innovative, Sustainable and Resilient Business*, London: Kogan Page

Jackson, B. & Parry, K. (2011) *A Very Short, Fairly Interesting and Reasonably Cheap Book about Studying Leadership*, London: Sage

Kallinokos, J. (2003) Work, Human Agency and Organisational Forms: An Anatomy of Fragmentation, *Organisation Studies*, May, 24(4): 595–618

Keats, J. (1899) *The Complete Poetical Works and Letters of John Keats*, Cambridge: Houghton-Mifflin

Kenny, I. (1999) *Freedom and Order: Studies in Strategic Leadership*, Dublin: Oak Tree Press

Lawrence, T., Mauws, M., Dyck, B. & Kleysen, R. (2005) The Politics of Organisational Learning: Integrating Power into the 4I Framework, *Academy of Management Review*, 30(1): 180–191

Local Government Association (2016) *LGA Corporate Peer Challenge: An Introduction to the Peer Challenge Process and the Role of Peers*, London: LGA

Maccoby, M. (2004) Why People Follow the Leader: The Power of Transference, *Harvard Business Review*, 82(9): 76–85

Malby, B. (2007) *How To Develop Leadership in the Public Sector – What Works For Organisational Effectiveness?: A Set of Design Principles for Providers and Commissioners of Leadership Interventions*, Leeds: Centre for Innovation in Health Management, University of Leeds/Northern Leadership Academy

Marsick, V. & Watkins, K. (1997) Lessons from Informal and Incidental Learning, in Burgoyne, J. & Reynolds, M. (Eds.) *Management Learning: Integrating Perspectives in Theory and Practice*, London: Sage

McCallum, S. & O'Connell, D. (2009) Social Capital and Leadership Development: Building Stronger Leadership through Enhanced Relational Skills, *Leadership & Organisation Development Journal*, 30(2): 152–166

Memon, A. & Kinder, T. (2015) Management in an Increasingly Collaborative and Integrated Public Sector: The Changing Managerial Role in the Scottish National Health

Service and the Implications for Managerial Learning and Development, *International Journal of Public Administration*, 39(4): 1–14

Miller, R. (2018) *Developing Integrated Care: The Role of the Multidisciplinary Team*, London: Social Care Institute for Excellence

Monbiot, G. (2016) Neoliberalism: The Ideology at the Root of All our Problems, *Guardian*, 15 April

Owen, H. (1997) *Open Space Technology: A User's Guide*, 2nd edition, San Francisco: Berrett-Koehler

Page, S. (2007) Making the Difference: Applying a Logic of Diversity, *Academy of Management Perspectives*, November: 6–20

Pedler, M., Warburton, D., Wilkinson, D., Spencer, N. & Wade, D. (2007) *Improving Poor Environments: The Role of Learning Architectures in Developing and Spreading Good Practice*, Bristol: Environment Agency

Pendleton, D. (2018) Leadership Jazz: Developing the Agile Organisation, Workshop presentation at Bristol International Jazz and Blues Festival, 16 March

Petrie, N. (2014) *Vertical Leadership Development: Part 1: Developing Leaders for a Complex World*, Greensboro, NC: Center for Creative Leadership

Petrie, N. (2015) *The How-To of Vertical Leadership: Part 2: 30 Experts, 3 Conditions and 15 Approaches*, Greensboro, NC: Center for Creative Leadership

Pratt, J., Plamping, D. & Gordon, P. (2003) Conversational Conferences: From Ideas to Action, *British Journal of Healthcare Management*, 9(3): 98–103

Raelin, J. (2008) Emancipatory Discourse and Liberation, *Management Learning*, 39(5): 519–540

Raelin, J. (2011) From Leadership-As-Practice to Leaderful Practice, *Leadership*, 7(2): 195–211

Raelin, J. (2018) What Are You Afraid of?: Collective Leadership and its Learning Implications, *Management Learning*, 49(1): 59–66

Revans, R. (1971) *Developing Effective Managers: A New Approach to Business Education*, London: Longman

Rock, D. (2008) SCARF: A Brain-Based Model for Collaborating with and Influencing Others, *Neuroleadership Journal*, 1

Rogers, C. (2007) *Informal Coalitions: Mastering the Hidden Dynamics of Organisational Change*, Basingstoke: Palgrave Macmillan

Ross, L. (1977) The Intuitive Psychologist and His Shortcomings: Distortions in the Attribution Process, in Berkowitz, L. (Ed.) *Advances in Experimental Social Psychology*, New York: Academic Press

Schon, D. (1983) *The Reflective Practitioner: How Professionals Think in Action*, London: Temple Smith

Senge, P., Roberts, C., Smith, B., Kleiner, A. & Ross, R. (1994) *The Fifth Discipline Fieldbook: Strategies and Tools for Building a Learning Organisation*, New York, NY: Doubleday

Thorpe, R., Gold, J., Anderson, L., Burgoyne, J., Wilkinson, D. & Malby, B. (2008) *Towards 'Leaderful' Communities in the North of England: Stories from the Northern Leadership Academy*, 2nd edition, Cork, Ireland: Oak Tree Press

Vince, R. & Pedler, M. (2018) Putting the Contradictions Back into Leadership Development, *Leadership & Organisation Development Journal*, 39(7): 859–872

Walmsley, J. & Miller, K. (2008) *A Review of the Health Foundation's Leadership Programmes: 2003–2007*, London: The Health Foundation

Weisbord, M. & Janoff, S. (1995) *Future Search: An Action Guide to Finding Common Ground in Organisations and Communities*, San Francisco: Berrett-Koehler

West, M. & Lyubovnikova, J. (2013) Illusions of Teamwork In Health Care, *Journal of Health Organisation & Management*, 27(1): 134–142

West, M. (2012) *Effective Teamwork: Practical Lessons from Organisational Research* (3rd edition), Oxford: Blackwell Publishing

Wheatley, M. (2007) *Finding Our Way: Leadership for an Uncertain Time*, San Francisco: Berrett-Koehler

Wilhelm, W. (2005) *Learning Architectures: Building Individual and Organisational Learning*, New Mexico: GCA Press

Wilkinson, D. (2009) *Next Generation Chief Executive Programme: Evaluation Report*, Leeds: Centre for Innovation in Health Management, University of Leeds

Wilson, S., Davison, N. & Casebourne, J. (2016) *Local Public Service Reform: Supporting Learning to Integrate Services and Improve Outcomes*, London: Institute for Government

4

SYSTEMS LEADERS LEADING CHANGE

This chapter seeks to identify what is wrong with current approaches to change management in health and social care and explores what an alternative would look like, with particular emphasis on how change can be effectively sustained and spread, before considering the practical applications of such an approach. It also acknowledges that change induces anxiety and considers what can be done to address this.

What's wrong with change management?

Health and social care organisations have historically been marked by regular (some might even say constant) changes to their structures and roles through reorganisations, restructurings, re-design, reconfigurations, downsizing and re-engineering, so that it is certainly understandable (and probably quite excusable) that there exists in many of the staff who work in them a feeling that change is being foisted on them – and hence they display a sense of weariness and 'change fatigue' and of a wary scepticism, often bordering on cynicism, with regard to the changes which systems leadership potentially implies. Such attitudes, which can act as a drag factor on change, can often be exacerbated by the so-called 'guru literature' outlined by some academic sources and by management consultancies. Indeed, it has been suggested that: 'the undue intervention of experts carrying no personal responsibility for the real life actions … is, at best, ambiguous, in general opinionative, and at worst, reactionary' (Revans, 2011).

However, the original causes of these attitudes may well lie in those approaches which have previously been adopted for leading change (Edmonstone, 1995), and which have typically been:

- Programmatic in nature. That is, episodic, project management-based and with a distinct beginning, middle and end (Beer et al., 1990). The ubiquity of project management in particular as a means of managing change has increasingly been criticised as being a 'cookbook' or 'recipe' approach which denies the messy real-world complexity, the dependence upon local circumstances and the over-riding centrality of working relationships (Ham et al., 2007). The study which made these criticisms also concluded that the NHS in particular 'needs to think beyond projects and towards more systemic shifts in processes and attitudinal and behavioural change.' When a piece of change work is externally funded, there is also a significant bureaucracy usually associated with managing the reporting demands of the funders. The underlying assumptions behind the programmatic approach would seem to be that it is entirely possible to agree on all pre-planned objectives at the outset of a change activity; that it is possible to agree on all the means by which those objectives can be assured, and that it is possible to accurately measure and assess the final outcome of such a project (Edmonstone, 1988). The assumption is therefore that change can be completely planned in advance and is linear in nature. This view is grounded in the machine metaphor for organisations described in Chapter 1. Reflecting this orientation, a few years ago in a review of the Organisation Development (OD) function in the NHS it was concluded that:

the NHS management community is so accustomed to a programmatic approach to change that they have become deskilled and are dependent on tools and programmes to improve things. Within such a culture of dependence, where all change is micro-managed and centrally-programmed, NHS managers are not at liberty to evaluate change, to reframe experience and to develop reflexive processes.

(Hardacre, 2005)

- 'Bracketed-off' and hence appearing to be separate and distinct from the ongoing and everyday processes of professional and managerial practice.
- Embodying a set of conscious and unconscious hierarchical assumptions, such as the supposed need to 'cascade' change from senior to lower hierarchical levels. Underlying this is the taken-for-granted acceptance of a so-called unitary frame of reference (Fox, 1973), suggesting that there is only one single source of (managerial) authority in an organisation, with only one focus of loyalty (the employer) and the existence of a single set of common shared objectives (embodied in such features as mission statements, business cases and plans, and performance management arrangements). In fact, both professional and managerial authority and loyalty co-exist and there are often multiple (and sometimes conflicting) personal and professional objectives.
- Assuming that change is best brought about by normative/re-educative strategies (Chin, 1969), sometimes known as 'training people into submission' (Edmonstone & Havergal, 1995) This assumes that changes

in people's knowledge and attitudes brought about by education and training programmes will then automatically lead to consequential changes in their behaviour – that, as a result of such programmes they will effectively think themselves into a new way of acting.

- An encouragement of 'representational learning' or the acquisition of the latest leadership and management jargon and acronyms, so that people simply learn to 'talk a good game' (Edmonstone, 2016) and to reframe their language without reframing their professional and/or managerial practice.
- Ignoring the gap between 'espoused theory' (or what people at work say that they do) and their 'theory-in-use' (what it is that they actually do in practice) (Argyris & Schon, 1974).
- Embodying an orientation towards conformist innovation (or small-scale and incremental change within a set of clearly-defined and prescribed boundaries), rather than deviant innovation (concerned with a reframing of the status quo and with what might possibly come next) (Legge, 1978).
- Most linear change management models are predicated on analysis and logic. They give the illusion of control to the senior management of organisations, but bypass the complex human dynamics and ignore the feelings of anxiety which change engenders (Carter & Varney, 2018). The way that employees feel about change at work may be influenced more by their own attitudes towards change in general, rather than by the merits or otherwise of specific changes. The latter are typically expressed only in rational and logical terms and it has been claimed that:

  - Most change agents rely primarily on rational approaches to foster organisational change.
  - Most change initiatives actually involve significantly non-rational dynamics and processes.
  - Most change agents still insist on operating as if organisational change is a purely rational process (Marshak, 2006).

What's the alternative?

Although variation is crucial in ensuring that public services meet local needs, not learning from what has been tried before, or tried elsewhere in the UK or internationally, is costly, time-intensive, and risks duplicating the progress made in other places. Therefore, re-inventing the wheel is really not a viable option. An alternative approach to leading change is therefore an essential element of systems leadership. This is likely to be based upon the following:

- A starting assumption that reality is 'messy' and that the wicked problems associated with integrating health and social care cannot be addressed using those methods which were devised to work on tame problems.

- A belief that transformational change is far more emergent than planned.
- Persistent and consistent support and challenge for change from the most senior influential people within the existing hierarchical arrangements within all the stakeholder organisations.
- An awareness of the wider context within which people are working, involving the framework of national policies and initiatives and including how their own and other stakeholder organisations work, who and what needs to be influenced and how best to do this.
- An acceptance of 'variable geometry' (or a recognition that there are diverse approaches to the same destination) and 'variable speed' (that there will be different rates of progress in different places).
- Rather than following a rigid methodology, insofar as project management is used, it needs to become much more exploratory, tentative and incremental (Edmonstone,, 2010).
- A shielding of local activity from national 'initiative-itis', that is, non-participation in those diversionary schemes which would mean little or nothing to key staff.
- Dropping any generic, a-cultural and packaged approaches to change for designs and approaches that are specific and wholly sensitive to the local context and culture.
- An expectation that there will be unexpected surprises and that new questions will arise along the way, which were certainly not foreseen at the outset.
- Rather than a predetermined single aim or purpose, the emphasis might well be placed on simply getting started with some joint action without fully agreeing on any ultimate aims, by establishing a 'working path' (Huxham & Vangen, 2005). This is because it may not always be possible to get complete agreement on such matters at the outset. The guiding image is that of a compass, rather than a route map. Key leaders may have to agree to walk together for some of the way without agreement on a final destination, not least because the path is likely to change over time as leaders learn more and find new ways to do things. The shared endeavour is the journey and defining the journey takes both time and care. As the Spanish poet Antonio Machado (2007) has suggested:

Life is the path you beat while you walk it.

It is the walking that beats the path.

It is not the path that makes the walk.

- Rather than a multitude of stand-alone actions, the development of a learning architecture or 'suite' of mutually-supportive activities which have a multiplier effect by feeding-off and reinforcing each other.

- An assumption that real (as opposed to short-term and cosmetic) change will take much longer than most people will ever anticipate. That it is quite definitely a marathon, and not just a sprint.
- An acceptance that there will, over time, need to be concomitant changes in the performance, reward and recognition systems, as form eventually comes to follow function.
- Promotion and adequate resourcing of multi-agency teams, with a sense of momentum for team working established and maintained through time.
- Wherever crucial, keeping such teams together and intact over realistic time-periods – and so potentially restricting assumptions regarding the rapid career movement of team members.
- 'Amplifying' success by offering emerging good practice as models from which others can learn, with the caveat that local circumstances may differ.
- Sufficient attention needs to be given to processes of review, evaluation and learning so, as well as any pre-set milestones, there will also be 'emergent' milestones – key activities which can only be identified retrospectively by such a review process.
- The structural and steering arrangements need to be 'a little bit more than not enough' – that is, just robust enough and sufficient to allow adequate exploration of the unknown and not to constrain initiative.
- Building relationships and rapport between key stakeholders needs to be much more important than any rigid adherence to deadlines. Change happens at the speed of trust.
- Managing the expectations of key stakeholders so that their expectations do not either move too far ahead of, or fall behind, the capability of the system to change.
- Abandoning one-off, persistent and inflexible 'solutions' for learn-as-we-go approaches, which embody the flexibility to change as events unfold and as learning about what does and does not work well becomes available. Allowing the overall strategy to increasingly emerge from successful actions and activities. Building from the ground up and being opportunistic and incremental with a strong focus on action, experimentation and innovation. This implies non-reliance upon those large national management consultancies who offer such packaged solutions, as recent research on the impact of such bodies working in the NHS indicates that they have not significantly improved efficiency at all (Kirkpatrick et al., 2018). Instead, as Revans (2011) suggested, the major difference is to encourage people to 'act themselves into a new way of thinking, rather than think themselves into a new way of acting'.

Ensuring sustainability and spread

There is now ample evidence concerning what is required in order to ensure both *sustainability* (that is, keeping the systems leadership storyline ongoing and preventing any diversions) and *spread* (or avoiding systems leadership from being 'contained' within existing command-and-control frameworks) in order to achieve desirable change (Buchanan et al., 2007).

Sustainability involves ensuring that systems leadership is perceived as central to the effectiveness and survival of the local system and all its elements. It can be ensured by:

- A clear, consistent and challenging vision of what is needed.
- Keeping the focus firmly on the needs of service users and the local population.
- Guaranteeing support at all levels and within all partner organisations and groups.
- Making certain that the importance and achievements of systems leadership are well-communicated consistently and over time, with the benefits being well-publicised.
- Highlighting the importance of flexible adaptation of change to suit local circumstances.
- Maintaining an ongoing sense of momentum.
- Recognition of achievements made and continuing support through processes of selection, appraisal, promotion and reward.
- Education and training activities which are tailored to both stimulate and support change.
- An increasing sense of teamwork being the norm or 'the way we do things round here'.
- A culture of confronting 'difficult' decisions, rather than one of avoiding them.
- Stability of leadership.

Spread involves:

- Accepting that the whole process inevitably takes time.
- A continuing focus on the use of personal and professional networks, key opinion-leaders and the centrality of interpersonal influence.
- The importance of 'selling' benefits, not just to the most obvious people, but also to those who are 'below the radar' – the quiet and influential leaders.
- Emphasising that the actions involved are part of 'swimming with the tide' of change, rather than against it.

Application

Applying these broad principles to the specifics of systems leadership and the integration of health and social care, a number of key messages have been identified (Dalton et al., 2015):

- Citizens and service users must always be at the heart of any systems change. It is about co-creation, not about consultation on a pre-prepared and given blueprint. It is really important not to lose sight of this when both local and national politics and conflicting priorities may be prevalent.
- Systems leadership is all about collective endeavour and shared purpose. So it is importantly about working 'off-line' and 'below the radar' – having conversations that lead to real work being done, as well as in more formal and structured ways.
- Getting the right people into the room so that the system is adequately represented is vital in any systems leadership intervention. By definition, the right people includes citizens, service users and their carers, as well as stakeholder organisations. When service providers see things from a service user perspective there can be 'penny-dropping' moments leading to enhanced awareness and understanding of issues and of the potential barriers to change.
- When the right people are in the room it is the key role of leadership in complex health and social care systems to ask questions, and definitely not to provide previously-derived pat answers. Using the multiple perspectives and the collective intelligence which are available in the room is vital.
- There is a need for the mutual involvement of both 'strategists' and 'doers'. The former find it easier to see the longer-term goals and feel able to give things away where appropriate, to act with magnanimity and to recognise the needs of partner organisations. The latter are operational people who share systems leadership values and skills, but who are more focused on getting on with the practical tasks. The two also need to be really well-connected and in continuing dialogue with each other.
- It is important to resist the urge to jump to instant, technical or off-the-shelf approaches in whole or in part or to rush quickly into a pilot stage. It is much better to focus initially on building relationships, trust and a shared understanding of the underlying issues.
- The testing-out of ideas may best initially be done using small, contained and 'fail-safe' experiments, based on the context of the here and now. These might possibly then move on to consider a strategic imperative or a 'burning platform' issue.
- The evidence base for taking the long-term view needs to be built. It is best to be prepared for things to take time. Nerve needs to be kept, together with adaptation as things change and a sense of momentum needs to be maintained.
- It will be necessary to develop incomplete, partial, clumsy and emergent ways forward.
- Systems leadership implies sharing leadership responsibility. Consequently, systems leaders support other people across a system to achieve greater things than they would have been able to do on their own.

A study of the diffusion of innovation (Albury et al., 2011) concluded that it:

does not occur rapidly and effectively within stable, rigid, hierarchical systems. Diffusion requires a level of instability and fluidity where new innovative practices can displace more traditional ways of working. Leaders ... need to encourage informed and well-managed risk-taking and counter embedded cultures of risk aversion.

It has been pointed out (Obolensky, 2014) that most people at the 'top' of hierarchical organisations simply do not know the innovative ways forward in addressing the wicked problems and challenges which their organisations face. They (the 'top' people) also know that they do not know, but cannot say that they do not know. This is because there is an expectation (both by themselves and also by others) that they should know. So they often pretend to know. Similarly, people at the front-line of those organisations do often know the most useful ways forward – and also know that the people at the 'top' do not know what they are. They also often know that the people at the 'top' know that they (the people at the 'top') do not know – but they still expect the 'top' to know! This is because it absolves those at the front-line of any culpability for what may be going wrong.

Faced with breaking out from this gridlock, Huxham and Vangen (2005) suggest that there are four activities which are vital to ensuring successful application. They are:

Embracing the right kind of people:

- Embracing all those who would like to be involved when the representation of partner stakeholders is problematic.
- Embracing all those who are needed or required, although some may possibly initially be reluctant.
- Fostering collaborative activity even in those situations where some members may not be fully 'on board' at the outset.

Empowering members to enable systems leadership:

- Creating an infrastructure through which all members can be enabled to participate in spite of their inevitable differences in skills and knowledge levels.
- Keeping communications flowing effectively when members are physically, organisationally, professionally and culturally dispersed.
- Providing specific and tailored help to individuals and groups where that support is needed.

Involving and supporting all members:

- Involving all members although they may have unequal role and power positions within organisational hierarchies.

- Equalising the commitment to all members, even though personal position might be strongly linked to only one organisation.
  Mobilising members to make things happen:
- Encouraging members to work on behalf of the system while recognising that they may also need something back in return.
- Moving the overall systems leadership agenda forward when members' intra-organisational incentives might possibly pull in different directions.
- Energising members even though they might well have different levels of commitment.
- Mobilising activity even though some members might well be less-informed or even ill-informed.

Revans (2011) put it much more succinctly as 'Doubt ascending speeds wisdom from above'. In overly performance-driven organisations, however, it is often the case that, by contrast, 'Doubt ascending speeds retribution from above'! So change really needs to be a combination of top-down, bottom-up and middle-out.

Addressing anxiety

Change makes many people anxious. Reactions to change, as previously highlighted, are not solely rational or intellectual processes, not least because professional and managerial systems leaders will have, in the past, personally experienced both positive and negative reactions to change which they will view inevitably through the template of their own emotional and psychological history. Such experiences will have been shaped and conditioned through family, work, professional, organisational and social groupings and have been influenced by other broader economic, social and political forces operating in both their employing organisations and in the wider society.

Attempting to change things inevitably always involves risk – of success, but also of failure. Thus, it always also involves anxiety. Anxiety can get in the way of trying something new and examples of anxiety-induced behaviour include:

- *A reluctance to join in:* An unwillingness to be creative in terms of personal behaviour and ideas. A reluctance to ask the 'What if...?' questions.
- *A narrow self-view:* A low self-assessment of individual abilities and resources with a resulting 'resource myopia' – an inability or unwillingness to recognise the valuable personal contribution that might be made.
- *Fear of losing face:* Worry about being perceived as having admitted to personal or professional incompetence or having backed down.
- *Fear of recrimination:* Because colleagues might misunderstand changed behaviour and so get angry or resentful.
- *Fear of losing control:* And making matters worse than they might already seem to be.

- *Fear of failure:* In the eyes of colleagues in their own and other organisations. People who fear the possibility of failure experience difficulty in taking even calculated risks will most likely undervalue the importance of emotions and will often not be spontaneous in their interactions with others.
- *Fear of ambiguity:* An avoidance of those matters which lack clarity or where possible outcomes are unknown or unpredictable. A reluctance to try something out, to see whether it works or not, and an overemphasis on the known at the expense of the unknown.
- *Fear of disorder:* A dislike of complexity (often labelled as 'confusion') and a preference for order, structure and balance, often expressed in terms of opposites, such as good versus bad or right versus wrong, with a corresponding failure to appreciate and integrate the best from such seemingly polarised viewpoints.
- *Fear of looking foolish:* And attracting negative comments from colleagues as having acted 'out of character'.
- *Fear of being vulnerable:* Of not really knowing what will happen as a result of trying a different approach.
- *Fear of letting someone else make a big mistake:* When feeling responsible for what the other person or persons do.
- *Fear of influencing others:* A concern not to appear aggressive or 'pushy' and hence a hesitation in identifying with emerging points of view.

The sources of such anxiety may also include an individual system leader's professional or managerial work role and the particular professional and organisational setting in which they operate, together with the specific nature of the issue or challenge on which they are working.

Such in-built immunities to change often lead to avoidance behaviour or to 'defensive routines' (Argyris, 1985) – unconscious strategies for self-protection, which unfortunately inhibit the potential to learn and so to become more effective. Such defensive thoughts and feelings will have been acquired over time and through personal experience because it is believed that they keep us safe but, incongruously, they are very often the source of failure – the very reason that people seem to remain stuck in stultified behaviour patterns.

Such defensive routines may include:

- *Spending time in inconclusive deliberations:* While many health and social care leaders would claim that they experienced a lack of time, this means that such people feel too heavily loaded with urgent tasks to engage in any kind of reflective activity. Yet such people also tend to feel frustrated by the amount of time which is spent in endless, unproductive or unsatisfactory meetings where decisions are not reached or where the same issues permanently recur.
- *Believing that everything is urgent:* The amount of wasted time spent in such meetings also ratchets up the sense of urgency and so, in turn, reduces the

willingness to be more reflective. Meetings usually have such tight agendas that there is little or no time left for any in-depth exploration of issues.

- *Surface-skimming:* Deeper reflection may be further avoided because it would mean exposing and experiencing a situation as being much more complex than was originally envisaged, so increasing the level of frustration and anxiety. It is not possible to fit the complexities and unpredictability associated with integrated working into an idealised and rational model as they are, by their very nature, messy. This can feel highly disturbing, especially for those people who are dominated by a need to feel always in control. Attempts may be made to minimise such discomfort by reducing complexity through ever-tighter controls and even more focus on desired targets. This then misses opportunities for deeper learning that can create greater clarity with regard to the possible choices which might be available. It can also lead to misunderstandings, as there is insufficient space and time to inquire into the underlying concepts and assumptions.

- *Avoiding decisions:* If a decision feels risky and there is not an environment that supports innovation and learning from mistakes, the result may be risk-averse behaviour and an avoidance of making decisions. It is the area of the 'definite maybe' and of the 'waver game' where a group cycles back and forth between two or more alternative decisions without ever coming to a final decision. When they almost get there, they immediately flip back to the opposite possibility.

Anxiety can therefore have destructive or self-limiting effects, but can also potentially provide the energy which is needed in order to risk being honest, direct, challenging and different. Confronting anxiety may involve individuals relinquishing their earlier roles, ideas and practices, in order to create, find or discover new and more adaptable ideas, ways of thinking and acting, and to cope with the instability of changing conditions and the insecurity which change always provokes. This is the process of 'unlearning' whereby well-established patterns of thinking and behaviour are interrupted and breached and redundant mind-sets are re-evaluated, re-positioned and embodied within a wider repertoire of possible responses. It is not simply about forgetting, but paradoxically is concerned with advancing by slowing down, stepping back and letting go from prior understanding that may limit the future (Brook et al., 2016).

One other way of dealing with anxiety is to seek sanctuary in the views of 'experts' (as described in Chapter 2). Such people seem to provide anxiety-reducing answers and so offer what can seem like safety and security. This is often the realm of management consultants and they may seem to offer 'magic bullets' to resolve the challenges of integrating health and social care services. It is, however, a false prospectus, because ultimately there is no real alternative to systems leaders owning, focusing and working on their own problems – with all the messiness, confusion and uncertainty which that entails. Rather than simply directly appropriating someone else's approach people instead need to experiment and develop their own ways forward or to 'flex' those approaches developed elsewhere to suit local circumstances. This is not at all easy, but can be achieved by acknowledging publicly at the outset that anxiety is probably likely to be present as people from different professions and organisations work together and by modelling the legitimate and measured expression of anxiety at all times.

By acting as a systems leader and emphasising the paramountcy of the health and social care system some individuals may find themselves adhering to a set of values which may differ from the dominant culture of their organisations. This positions them on the boundary – effectively both inside and outside of their organisations – as a basis for their thinking and actions. As such they are acting as 'tempered radicals', that is: 'People who want to succeed in their organisations, yet want to live by their values or identities, even if they are somehow at odds with the dominant culture of their organisations' (Myerson, 2003).

Such people do want to fit in organisationally, but also want to retain what it is that makes them different from their colleagues. It is very much an ambivalent position and requires a careful balancing act on the part of the individual concerned in deciding, for example, what course of action to pursue, how far to push and when to hold back (Myerson & Scully, 1995).

The dangers which tempered radicals have to guard against include (Brookfield, 1994):

- A possible sense of despair at the implications of them adopting what may appear to their peers as a radical analysis with respect to their professional or organisational context.
- A developing feeling of 'lost innocence' as they increasingly come to question their own taken-for-granted assumptions.
- A growing feeling of 'impostership' as they may doubt their own worthiness to question their own organisation or profession – or even both.
- Experiencing a feeling of 'cultural suicide' as they encounter the disbelief and possible hostility of their colleagues when they question or challenge the accepted professional and/or organisational practices.

Nevertheless, such tempered radicals are very often the catalysts for change as they act as 'boundary-spanners' between different organisations (Williams, 2011).

Finally, it is worth emphasising that the future simply cannot be predicted, but it can be envisioned and brought into being. Health and social care systems cannot ultimately be controlled, but they can be designed and re-designed. It is possible to listen to what the system tells us and to discover how its properties and values can work together to bring forth something much better than can ever be produced by any single individual, professional or organisational will alone (Meadows, 2008).

This chapter has identified major difficulties with the current approaches to leading and managing change in health and social care. It has offered an alternative approach and has examined the practical implications associated with application of such an approach. Recognising that change inevitably provokes anxiety, the manifestations of this have been described and ways of addressing it have been suggested. The particular pressures experienced by tempered radicals have been spotlighted.

References

Albury, D., Begley, A., Corrigan, P., Harvey, S. & McMahon, L. (2011) *After the Light Bulb: Accelerating Diffusion of Innovation in the NHS*, London: UCL Partners

Argyris, C. (1985) *Strategy, Change and Defensive Routines*, London: Pitman Publishing

Argyris, C. & Schon, D. (1974) *Theory in Practice: Increasing Professional Effectiveness*, San Francisco: Jossey-Bass

Beer, M., Einsenstat, R. & Spector, B. (1990) Why Change Programs Don't Produce Change, *Harvard Business Review.* November/December, 68(6): 158–166

Brook, C., Pedler, M., Abbott, C. & Burgoyne, J. (2016) On Stopping Doing Those Things that Are Not Getting Us to Where We Want to Be: Unlearning and Critical Action Learning, *Human Relations*, 69(2): 369–389

Brookfield, S. (1994) Tales from the Darkside: A Phenomenology of Adult Critical Reflection, *International Journal of Lifelong Education*, 13(3): 203–216

Buchanan, D., Fitzgerald, L. & Ketley, D. (2007) Sustaining Change and Avoiding Containment: Practice and Policy, in Buchanan, D., Fitzgerald, L. & Keteley, D. (Eds.) *The Sustainability and Spread of Organisational Change*, Abingdon: Routledge

Carter, A. & Varney, S. (2018) *Change Capability in the Agile Organisation*, Brighton: Institute for Employment Studies

Chin, R. (1969) The Utility of Systems Models and Developmental Models for Practitioners, in Bennis, W., Benne, K. & Chin, R. (Eds.) *The Planning of Change*, New York: Rinehart & Winston

Dalton, M., Jarvis, J., Powell, B. & Sorkin, D. (2015) *The Revolution Will Be Improvised: Part 2: Insights from Places on Transforming Systems*, London: The Leadership Centre

Edmonstone, J. (1988) A False God?: How Relevant Is Competency-Based Education and Training to the NHS?, *Health Services Management*, 84(6): 156–160

Edmonstone, J. (1995) Managing Change: An Emerging New Consensus, *Health Manpower Management*, 21(1): 16–19

Edmonstone, J. (2010) A New Approach to Project Managing Change, *British Journal of Healthcare Management*, 16(5): 114–119

Edmonstone, J. (2016) Leadership Metaphors, *Leadership in Health Services*, 29(2): 118–121

Edmonstone, J. & Havergal, M. (1995) The Death (and Rebirth?) of Organisation Development, *Health Manpower Management*, 21(1): 28–33

Fox, A. (1973) Industrial Relations: A Social Critique of Pluralist Ideology, in Child, J. (Ed.) *Man And Organisation*, London: Allen & Unwin

Ham, C., Parker, H., Singh, D. & Wade, E. (2007) *Beyond Projects: Case Studies from the Care Closer to Home: Making the Shift Programme*, Birmingham: NHS Institute for Innovation & Improvement/Health Services Management Centre, University of Birmingham

Hardacre, J. (2005) How Does the NHS Interpret and Use OD?, MSc Thesis, University of Birmingham

Huxham, C. & Vangen, S. (2005) *Managing to Collaborate: The Theory and Practice of Collaborative Advantage*, Abingdon: Routledge

Kirkpatrick, I., Sturdy, A., Alvarado, N., Blanco-Oliver, A. & Veronesi, G. (2018) The Impact of Management Consultants on Public Service Efficiency, *Policy & Politics*, 46(2): 1–19

Legge, K. (1978) *Power, Innovation and Problem-Solving in Personnel Management*, Maidenhead: McGraw-Hill

Machado, A. (2007) *Fields of Castile*, Translated by S. Appelbaum, Chatham: Dover Publications

Marshak, R. (2006) *Covert Processes at Work: Managing the Five Hidden Dimensions of Organizational Change*, San Francisco, CA: Berrett-Koehler

Meadows, D. (2008) *Thinking in Systems: A Primer*, White River Junction, VT: Chelsea Green

Myerson, D. (2003) *Tempered Radicals: How Everyday Leaders Inspire Change at Work*, Boston: Harvard Business School Press

Myerson, D. & Scully, M. (1995) Tempered Radicals and the Politics of Radicalism and Change, *Organisation Science*, 6(5): 585–600

Obolensky, N. (2014) *Complex Adaptive Leadership: Embracing Paradox and Uncertainty*, 2nd edition, Farnham: Gower

Revans, R. (2011) *ABC of Action Learning*, Farnham: Gower

Williams, P. (2011) The Life and Times of the Boundary Spanner, *Journal of Integrated Care*, 19(3): 26–33

5

THE CHALLENGE OF EVALUATING SYSTEMS LEADERSHIP

While it is clear that systems leadership forms the direction of travel towards the destination of integrated health and social care services, it will be important to evaluate and review that journey and to learn from the experience, not least for the purposes of effective steering. Traditionally, evaluations of development activity have depended largely upon the impressions formed by individual leaders, often surveyed after the particular event or events concerned in which they had participated. Such an approach makes it difficult to form an accurate impression of any real impact that such development activities may have on the system. This is partly because of the retrospective nature of such evaluations and also due to a (perhaps inevitable) 'rosy glow' that surrounds the recollections of events through which individuals and groups may have passed.

Problems with evaluation

While there is almost universal agreement on the importance and value of evaluation, ample evidence suggests that many developmental activities and processes continue to follow, one after the other, with little evaluation of their impact before there is a transition on to the next activity (Hirsh et al., 2011). This is particularly true in the public sector, where national initiatives are often 'cascaded' in a hierarchical manner into local settings and where evaluation of the success, or otherwise, of such initiatives is particularly rare, perhaps because such evaluation might result in an 'unacceptable finding' which could potentially be career-limiting to those associated with the particular initiative.

The standard approach to evaluation (Kirkpatrick & Kirkpatrick, 1998) is based upon the following model, where data is collected on:

- *Reactions:* To an event or events in the form of individuals' thoughts and feelings. This is the level of the 'happy sheet' administered to a captive audience at the end of an event and is the most common form of assessment used.

It is slightly more difficult, although not impossible, to also collect data on

- *Learning:* That is, to what degree have individuals acquired or changed the intended knowledge, skills and attitudes, based upon their involvement in an event?

It is even more problematic to collect data on resulting behavioural changes in performance.

- *Behaviour:* To what degree do individuals actually apply what they have learned when they are back in their job and organisational setting?

Finally, it is difficult indeed to collect data on:

- *Outcomes or results:* To what degree do targeted outcomes occur as a result of an event or events – in other words, what is the effect of changed behaviour on organisational performance?

The movement from reactions through learning and behaviour to outcomes introduces a significant number of intervening variables (or other things happening to an individual or group and going on within an organisation) which make it more difficult (and some would even suggest impossible) to ascribe a simple linear cause-and-effect relationship. Furthermore, the correlation between the levels described is weak because a positive result at one level (such as reactions) does not automatically translate into a positive result at the next level (such as learning). Over-concentration on the relatively easy to assess individual reactions tends to side-line the larger system-wide contextual factors.

A further popular approach to evaluation is the Return on Investment (ROI) methodology (Phillips & Phillips, 2008), developed from the 1980s. The key feature of ROI is the calculation of the monetary value of investing in a particular programme or activity. The results of such a programme or activity are converted into a financial value, enabling a cost-benefit analysis to take place. Those results which cannot be so monetised are called 'intangibles' or 'externalities' and in the ROI approach these have a secondary importance. With ROI only financial quantitative data really matters and intangibles/externalities, as evidenced by qualitative data, are thus relegated to this secondary role. The ROI approach therefore risks either minimising such qualitative results or forcing an essentially hypothetical and subjective financial value onto them. Yet such intangibles or externalities can, of course, potentially lead to significant benefits over time. This is because there are no such side effects, just effects, and the very notion of side effects is most likely a sign that the mental models associated with evaluation are too narrow, and the time horizons too short (Sterman, 2012).

There are also important difficulties with quantitative-only approaches to evaluation. They may be problematic for certain development activities (such as those where intangibles/externalities such as improved relationships are the focus) but also because to measure anything an objective yardstick is needed, such as centimetres for length, kilogrammes for weight and litres for volume. Human activity at work involves a range of complex tasks that are highly context-dependent and so it may well be a fallacy to believe that such activity can be measured objectively using a yardstick and thus result in 'hard' figures. Measurement of this kind often tends to use Likert scales, which involve questionnaire respondents rating a series of statements by selecting from a range of possible responses (such as Poor, Adequate, Good and Very Good) or figures (often -2, -1, 0, $+1$, $+2$). These are, of course, intuitive approximations based on subjective criteria and any translation of results into figures serves to create a false impression of objective quantifiability, and as a result such a process has been described as methodologically specious (Verhaeghe, 2014). The danger of making decisions based solely on quantitative data and ignoring qualitative matters is known as the McNamara Fallacy, named after the United States Secretary of Defense during the Vietnam War. It runs as follows:

> The first step is to measure whatever can be easily measured. This is OK as far as it goes. The second step is to disregard what can't be measured easily or to give it an arbitrary value. This is artificial and misleading. The third step is to presume that whatever can't be measured easily really isn't important. This is blindness. The fourth step is to say whatever can't be measured easily really doesn't exist. This is suicide.
>
> *(Yankelovich, 1972)*

A further possibility would be to adopt what has been called a 'counterfactual' approach (Hardacre et al., 2011) which involves the use of a team of evaluators, who would not be aware of, or associated with, the particular development activity, being used to investigate matters in a carefully choreographed 'blind' manner in order to ascertain:

- *What happened?* What kind of individual, group and system changes or improvements have recently taken place?
- *How did it happen and who was involved?* What changed behaviour and activity had been exhibited in delivering those changes or improvements?
- *What changes had been achieved and were they sustainable?* Whether these changes or improvements could be tracked back and so linked directly to the development activity.

However, the logistics of such an approach are highly complex and the potential costs of undertaking evaluation along such lines would be most likely to outweigh the potential benefits achieved.

For such reasons, in the most major recent review of evaluation for leadership and management development (Hirsh et al., 2011) the authors unsurprisingly recommended the combination of both qualitative and quantitative data.

The problems with these conventional approaches to evaluation can be summarised as follows:

- They focus completely on the experiences of individual leaders and managers, rather than on the collective system as a whole.
- They ignore the importance of the intangibles or externalities within the local context or setting.
- They over-value quantification at the expense of qualitative matters.

Problems with evaluating systems leadership

It should be noted at the outset that systems leadership is not an end in itself, but a means towards an end. The end is effective integrated health and social care for both individuals and communities. This can easily be lost sight of because of the growth of a leadership development 'industry', based on: 'the domination of leadership development professionals who have a particular position and a vested interest in promoting models based on development centres, psychometric testing and off-site events' (NHS Confederation, 2009).

As a result, much of the literature which is available relates almost solely to evaluation of *leader development*, rather than of leadership development, with the emphasis being on the individual leader rather than on the significant collective effort that systems leadership entails. Even when efforts are made to devise frameworks to evaluate systems leadership the almost inevitable individual focus often continues to predominate (O'Neill, 2016).

Systems leadership implies emergence, so that it is not possible to know at the outset exactly what the way forward will be nor the particular route that might be taken. It addresses wicked problems, creates new forms of complexity, involves the multiple perspectives of stakeholders and sees relationships as being key. It is unsuited to conventional 'training' approaches, which seek to constrain uncertainty and aim to establish order through curricula, best practices and set techniques (Pedler & Abbott, 2013). Approaches to evaluation of systems leadership therefore need to understand and accept this.

Systems leadership also works through *generative causation*, creating the conditions where things can change and move on to destinations yet unknown, rather than *successionist causation* or achieving predictable and pre-known outcomes (Pawson & Tilley, 1997). It is even questionable whether there is a final 'arrival point' and so evaluation can be seen as directed towards a moving target, and therefore perhaps only a series of evaluation 'snapshots' may realistically be possible.

It is helpful to distinguish between two different kinds of evaluation. Some evaluation activity is *formative* (or developmental) in nature. It is concerned with making things better, with steering and improving things while they are happening. As such, it serves to reinforce learning, as evaluation is a feedback loop which contributes to the learning process itself. The other major kind of evaluation is *summative* (or judgemental) and is concerned with attempting to assess the overall measurable impact or contribution made. Summative evaluation is typically favoured by funders, who prefer 'hard' data and value quick answers. By contrast, formative evaluation is favoured by developers who value the rich information accrued, including the impact of context or setting on learning and performance.

In evaluating systems leadership, it will be important to strike an appropriate balance between formative and summative approaches and between the collection and analysis of both qualitative and quantitative data. However, the major focus needs to be on formative evaluation because it serves to create a helpful feedback cycle and encourages learning and improvement.

A way forward

It is not the intention to prescribe a single framework for evaluating systems leadership, as this will obviously depend upon a number of factors in the local setting, such as:

- *Timing:* How to evaluate the development of systems leadership in the short-term, when the anticipated benefits are more likely to mature in the longer-term?
- *Complexity:* How to tease out the effects of certain developmental actions from those of others, given the multiplicity of intervening (and overlapping) variables which have previously been mentioned?
- *Value:* What is to be counted as 'success' and by whom? Given the multiple stakeholders in a local health and social care system this is a major issue.
- *Cost:* Conducting evaluation is not cost-free, either in finance or time. It may require additional finance and work to implement.
- *Horses for courses:* The size and complexity of any evaluation need to be in proportion to the particular activity or activities being evaluated.
- *Politics:* Evaluation is a complex and highly political process. The underlying assumption is that discovering 'what works' will simply result in evidence-based future action. However, policy decisions are often made despite the evidence of what does or does not work in practice. Evaluation can even be designed to gather data that supports a particular policy direction – that is, policy-based evidence, rather than evidence-based policy. If evaluation results are politically sensitive and come up with 'unacceptable findings' then they may never even be released publicly and may be ignored. Decisions are made based upon much more than the evidence from evaluation studies – values, interests, personalities, timing, circumstances and happenstance also play their parts.

Rather than offer a framework, instead a series of questions are offered which may assist with the local design of an evaluation process for systems leadership:

- Are the service user and the local community placed at the heart of the development of systems leadership?
- Are the changes which are taking place in the wider environment in which the local system exists being identified and adapted to?
- Are wicked problems really being addressed or is the focus only on tame problems or on the consideration of wicked problems as if they were tame?
- Are the diverse viewpoints of the multiple stakeholders in the system being sought, paid attention to and acted on?
- Is systems leadership being promoted and developed at all levels across the health and social care system – both horizontally and vertically?
- Is real and significant, rather than cosmetic, change being pursued?
- Are the inevitable conflicts which arise being addressed creatively?
- Are 'failures' being used as a means of learning, rather than in a punitive manner?
- Is there evidence of a growing system culture which combines both support and challenge to individuals and groups?
- Is the inevitable anxiety which change induces being recognised and addressed head-on?
- Is there evidence of a suite of development activities and associated funding in place to support, spread and sustain systems leadership?
- Is there evidence of processes of evaluation and review being conducted for the purpose of steering and learning?

There would inevitably be further supplementary questions arising from these and there would also be other questions more specifically related to the local context and to particular initiatives.

The ultimate test for systems leadership is that set out in the Introduction. Will it develop more collaborative, diverse, inclusive and outcome-focused approaches to integrated care, whilst seeking to maintain quality, compassion, financial balance and effective group and individual performance? Will it embody working together to mobilise the assets in the local community and the collective capabilities in order to improve the quality of health and social care for individuals and local populations, while also ensuring the wise stewardship of taxpayers' money? It is also worth pointing out that:

> Evaluation can only ever provide good quality information to inform decision-making. It is unlikely to supply ready-made answers because the results will need to be interpreted as part of a process of discussion and judgement, with the views of different stakeholders and the intended outcomes of the activity being taken into account.

> *(Larsen et al., 2005)*

References

Hardacre, J., Cragg, R., Shapiro, J., Spurgeon, P. & Flanagan, H. (2011) *"What's Leadership Got To Do with It?": Exploring Links between Quality Improvement and Leadership in the NHS*, London: ORCNI Ltd for the Health Foundation

Hirsh, W., Tamkin, P., Garrow, V. & Burgoyne, J. (2011) *Evaluating Management and Leadership Development: New Ideas and Practical Approaches*, Brighton: Institute for Employment Studies

Kirkpatrick, D. & Kirkpatrick, J. (1998) *Evaluating Training Programs: The Four Levels*, 4th edition, San Francisco, CA: Berrett-Koehler

Larsen, L., Cummins, J. & Brown, H. (2005) *Learning from Evaluation: Summary of Reports of Evaluations of Leadership Initiatives*, London: Office for Public Management/NHS Leadership Centre

NHS Confederation (2009) *Reforming Leadership Development .... Again*, London: NHS Confederation

O'Neill, P. (2016) *The Leadership Development Evaluation Framework: Developing Evidence-Based Interventions and Creating a Learning Culture*, Nottingham: East Midlands NHS Leadership Academy

Pawson, R. & Tilley, N. (1997) *Realistic Evaluation*, London: Sage

Pedler, M. & Abbott, C. (2013) *Facilitating Action Learning: A Practitioner's Guide*, Maidenhead: Open University Press

Phillips, J. & Phillips, P. (2008) *The Basics of ROI*, www.humanresourcesiq.com/hr-technol ogy/columns/the-basics-of-roi/

Sterman, J. (2012) Sustaining Sustainability: Creating a Systems Science in a Fragmented Academy and Polarised World, in Weinstein, M. & Turner, R. (Eds.), *Sustainability Science: The Emerging Paradigm and the Urban Environment*, New York: Springer Science

Verhaeghe, P. (2014) *What about Me?: The Struggle for Identity in a Market-Based Society*, London: Scribe Publications

Yankelovich, D. (1972) *Corporate Priorities: A Continuing Study of the New Demands on Business*, Stanford, CT: Daniel Yankelovich Inc.

6

FOUR JOURNEYS TO SYSTEMS LEADERSHIP

This chapter considers the four very different approaches to systems leadership in health and social care developed in the four parts of the UK – Scotland, Northern Ireland, Wales and England.

Scotland

Context

From around 2000 the NHS in Scotland has pursued an approach of increasing collaboration, partnership and integration, both within health care but more particularly between health and social care. The 2002 Community Care and Health (Scotland) Act conferred powers to transfer specific functions, without removing statutory responsibilities, together with an associated power to create pooled budgets between health and social care partners. Initially, voluntary combinations of General Practitioners (GPs) were encouraged to form *Local Health Care Co-operatives (LHCCs)* but from 2003 they evolved into *Community Health Partnerships (CHPs)* (some health-only, others covering both health and social care) accountable to both the local NHS Board and to the relevant local authority. A 2011 review of CHPs by Audit Scotland found that:

- They did not have the necessary authority required in order to implement the challenging integration agenda which they faced.
- There was a 'cluttered landscape' with CHPs added on to previously developed local partnership arrangements.
- There were major differences in organisational cultures, planning, performance and financial management regimes in health and social care.

Subsequently, in 2011 the Scottish Government pledged to deliver a single integrated system of health and social care across Scotland and proposed the replacement of the then 36 CHPs with 31 *Health and Social Care Partnerships (HSCPs)* which, through *Integration Joint Boards (IJBs)*, would be the joint responsibility of the fourteen territorial NHS Boards and the 32 local authorities and would oversee spending in excess of £8 billion. Localities, which are conceived as natural communities based on both geography and GP practices, were seen as the 'engine rooms of integration'. Each HSCP was to comprise of at least two localities.

Legislation in 2014 required Health Boards and local authorities to work in partnership with the third sector, users, carers and other key stakeholders, including the independent sector. Two optional models were suggested for integration, with the chosen model, best-suited to local need, to be agreed by the Health Board and local authority:

- *Option 1: Body Corporate:* Here the Health Board and local authority would delegate the responsibility for planning and resourcing service provision for adult health and social care services to an Integration Joint Board.
- *Option 2: Lead Agency:* Here either the Health Board or the local authority would take the lead responsibility for planning, resourcing and delivering integrated adult health and social care services.

The most favoured was Option 1 and the revised system then went live in April, 2016. An early review of these arrangements (Audit Scotland, 2015) identified the following issues:

- The pressing need for members of Integration Joint Boards to understand and respect the differences in organisational cultures and backgrounds and to manage conflicts of interest.
- Challenges in agreeing the budgets for the new HSCPs, in setting out their strategic plans and in developing workforce planning for an integrated health and social care workforce.
- An inadequacy of the existing performance measures and the linkage of such measures to desired outcomes.
- A lack of development of the localities.

A further study, which sought to learn from Scotland's experience (Dayan & Edwards, 2017), noted that there was in Scotland a generally more co-operative culture and legal framework supporting integration of services. In particular, there had been no major structural or organisational change in the NHS in Scotland for over 10 years. However, it also noted:

- The need for flexibility in considering exactly what localities should be.
- The centrality to success of effective working relationships and the importance of an 'organic', rather than a legal impetus to development.

Leadership development

Leadership development support for systems leadership comprises two complementary programmes which are offered as a joint partnership between the special (non-territorial) Health Board, NHS Education for Scotland, the Scottish Social Services Council and the Royal College of General Practitioners, Scotland.

The first, *You as a Collaborative Leader (YACL)*, is effectively an individual leader development activity. It is aimed at primary care and social care professionals, including General Practitioners, senior primary care professionals and middle or senior managers in statutory, third or independent social care organisations who are already working in lead roles within their localities or in Health and Social Care Partnerships to shape, develop and deliver integrated care. The programme is designed to help those participants to recognise their own leadership strengths and sources of resilience and to discover how best to use these to lead change more collaboratively and effectively in order to deliver health and social care integration. The purpose is to support the individual to create greater presence, to influence more effectively and to have greater impact as a collaborative leader. Fully-funded, the programme is completed over four months and involves:

- Three one-to-one coaching sessions at the beginning, middle and end of the four-month long programme.
- A 360-degree assessment and feedback exercise on personal leadership capability.
- Two full-day workshops focusing on leadership capabilities for health and social care integration, with some content on the vision for integrated care and on the people, contexts and systems that impact on leadership actions.
- A tailored personal development plan to help the individual to sustain this learning in practice.

As a result, the focus of the YACL programme is largely on personal reflection and role.

The second programme, *Collaborative Leadership in Practice (CLIP)*, is aimed at broadly the same target audience and is also fully-funded. The programme offers tailored support to enable groups or Partnerships to lead collaboratively and to move forward effectively with a particular project or issue that supports health and social care integration. Such projects can relate directly to Local Delivery Plans or may be evolving from other creative and innovative approaches within localities. The programme lasts for eight months and involves a Leadership for Integration team working in collaboration with the locality or Partnership group by:

- Supporting the locality or Partnership to develop the skills needed for effective collaboration.
- Giving the locality or Partnership supported time and space for them to work on the local actions, challenges and opportunities for health and social care integration.

- Helping the locality or Partnership to develop and apply skills, knowledge and understanding of the relevant issues in leadership, change, systems thinking and co-creating the future.

The flexibility of the programme – effectively a form of leadership development, as opposed to individual leader development – means that the appropriate bespoke support for each specific group can be co-designed and co-facilitated, with the potential elements including team coaching, Appreciative Inquiry, workshops, action learning and facilitated meetings within localities.

In a major evaluation of these programmes, Sharp (2018) indicated that:

- One hundred and forty-six people had taken part in five cohorts of YACL, each bringing their own live issues into coaching and workshop sessions, with the result that, whatever the immediate focus, the learning was both immediate and applied.
- The CLIP supporting project team had engaged with 52 different sites, across 21 HSCP areas. In 30 of those sites there had been bespoke coaching and facilitation interventions to develop local responses to integration and to address practical partnership issues. Because of the tailored nature of the programme, there was no such thing as a typical CLIP site. The participants were described as 'committed, caring, busy and practical people, who were also anxious, fragile and overloaded'. These interventions had enabled the exploration of common values and purposes and had also enabled health and social care professionals to talk much more openly and productively about their fears, anxieties and hopes for integration. The evaluation also identified many tangible and practical measures initiated by local CLIP groups
- The evaluation study concluded that:
  - These programmes had brought 'integration' to life for programme participants through immersion in what health and social care integration really meant locally, through engagement as active participants, rather than as spectators.
  - There were examples of changes in both thinking and practice that were significant as a demonstration of what was possible both currently and in the future, as well as providing much needed momentum and energy for further change.
  - Integration was everywhere a work in progress. Both programmes had been able, however, to challenge many dominant narratives, for example, the notion that integration was something 'imposed' upon people by statute and which might cause fear or anxiety about jobs, professional roles and the future of services. Instead it had been turned into something for which there was a more positive individual and collective commitment, because of the belief that it would ultimately improve outcomes for both people and communities.

- The new understandings and relationships that now existed amongst local professionals, teams and organisations, gave them confidence that they were working on the right track.

Northern Ireland

Context

Northern Ireland has had a structurally integrated system of health and social care since as long ago as 1973. It was created as a result of a local government reorganisation when social care was completely divested from local authorities and transferred at that time to four area *Health and Social Services Boards (HSSBs)*. Due to the period of direct rule from Westminster (between 1972 and 1999), and again in the periods when the Northern Ireland Assembly was suspended, much of the intervening period had been marked by a degree of stagnation in terms of further development.

In 2009 a single commissioning body, the *Health and Social Care Board (HSC)* (embodying five local commissioning groups), was created and the local commissioning groups were coterminous with five Health and Social Care Trusts. The Compton Review of 2011 highlighted the need for improved integration between health and social care, but there was a paucity of any evaluation or assessment of the existing integration arrangements. That Review proposed the creation of 17 locally-based *Integrated Care Partnerships (ICPs)*, described as cooperative networks of care providers with General Practitioners taking a critical leadership role.

One positive feature of the system was that of integrated management, with selection for programme manager and team leader positions in an integrated service open to a wide range of professions, but especially to nursing and social work staff. However, among the criticisms of the then current arrangements were that:

- Health care significantly dominated the policy agenda and there was not a real marriage of equal partners between health and social care.
- Core professional education and training took place in a 'siloed' manner and there was a worrying absence of inter-professional training.
- There had been a distinct lack of rigorous and robust evaluation and assessment of the system.
- As a result, the opportunities offered by some 45 years of integration had not been fully exploited.

The Donaldson Report (Donaldson et al., 2014), although again being largely health-oriented, highlighted:

- That traditional and bureaucratic approaches were still the norm in terms of everyday ways of working.
- That the commissioning of care was simply not working well.

- That the existing design of the health and social care system actually hindered high-quality and safe care.
- That the implementation of change was, as a result, exceedingly slow.

The 2016 Expert Panel Report (Department of Health, 2016b), although yet again very health-focused, noted that the health and social care workforce was still strongly siloed and largely felt disempowered. Innovation was significantly subordinated to 'fire-fighting' and crisis management and the proposed way forward was the development of *Accountable Care Systems (ACSs)* to integrate the provider sector, based on the existing Integrated Care Partnerships and the developing General Practitioner Federations. Such a movement would require 'new forms of systems leadership'.

Leadership development

A further report (Department of Health, 2016a) endorsed the need for collective and systems leadership at all levels and initiated the creation of a leadership strategy, which was published in 2017 (Department of Health, 2017). Subsequently, work has gone forward to articulate and develop a collective leadership capability framework, based on a set of core values and including a set of associated behaviours. In particular, the emphases will be on the development of trust, the ability to recognise and handle conflict and a commitment to work together for the longer term, rather than only on time-limited projects.

The *Health and Social Care Leadership Centre* acts as an internal consultancy service for health and social care in Northern Ireland, working (where appropriate) with higher education institutions. The programmes offered by the Centre will increasingly reflect the core values and associated behaviours developed as part of the collective leadership capability framework. In particular, these will include the following programmes:

Aspire: Targeted at senior managers the programme seeks to explore and build collaboration across a range of service areas. The programme is modular in nature and features action learning, coaching, team improvement and e-learning.

Proteus: Aimed at Assistant Directors and clinicians, the programme enhances the ability to engage and influence effectively across professional and organisational boundaries in a complex system. Modular in nature, the programme involves coaching, personal assessment, improvement and innovation tools.

Postgraduate Diploma in Health and Social Care Management: The programme aims to develop leaders and managers within health and social care and to assist them in planning, implementing and sustaining change in order to transform services. It is designed for middle and senior managers, including clinicians and professionals with management responsibilities, social work managers and managers in support functions. Participants need to have at least three years' appropriate management experience and to possess a first degree or equivalent or be able to demonstrate an ability to undertake the programme through their prior experiential learning. The programme features e-learning, action learning, tutorials and taught material.

All these programmes are individual leader development in nature, but the Leadership Centre also offers a range of bespoke organisation and management consultancy support to health and social care organisations in Northern Ireland.

Wales

Context

Health care is a devolved issue in Wales, as it is in Scotland and Northern Ireland. Since devolution there has been a continuing direction of travel away from the English quasi-market regime. Initially, 22 *Local Health Boards (LHBs)* which were coterminous with their 22 local authority counterparts commissioned health services from NHS Trusts. In 2009, however, there was a merger of all the health care commissioning and providing functions into seven LHBs who were tasked to work with the 22 local authorities (who provide social services), the police and the third sector through seven *Local Service Boards (LSBs)*, later re-badged *Public Service Boards (PSBs)*. These latter are not statutory bodies, but are intended to be expressions of local public service leadership. Their role is to coordinate action in priority areas where co-operation is most needed and expected to yield greatest results. Community health care was provided by some 64 *locality networks* – 'Clusters' of General Practitioner practices, pharmacists, and so on, which provide services for their local populations of between 30,000 and 50,000 people.

The major problems identified with these arrangements were (Ham et al., 2013):

- They remained with siloed (i.e. single-agency only) performance management measures.
- Those LHBs which had several local authorities to work with all experienced difficulties in co-ordinating planning and delivery.
- Multiple information systems existed and there was slow progress in developing common IT platforms.
- There was little patient and carer voice.
- There were very few shared budgets or shared appointments.
- There was evidence of cost-shunting behaviour between agencies.
- Long-standing professional loyalties were acting as a brake to change.
- A 'not invented here' risk-averse culture existed and there was a reluctance to adopt good practice which was sourced from elsewhere.
- 'Patchy' systems leadership existed but this was both fragile and unpredictable.

In 2016 seven statutory *Regional Partnership Boards (RPBs)* between local government, the third sector and the NHS were created to drive forward the strategic regional delivery of social services, in close collaboration with the NHS in Wales.

In 2017 *Social Care Wales (SCW)* was established to regulate and develop the Welsh social care workforce and to lead improvement to services and in 2018 *Health Education and Improvement Wales (HEIW)* was established.

The 2018 Parliamentary Review (Welsh Assembly, 2018) placed a strong emphasis on the further development of localities and on the need for Wales to learn from experience in both the other parts of the UK and internationally; it identified the need for joint inspection regimes and called for the development of performance management systems for integrated health and social care. The importance of leadership across the entire system, at all levels, was also strongly highlighted.

The Welsh Government's 2018 response to the Parliamentary Review identified a set of proposed whole system values, i.e.

- *Co-ordinating health and social care services seamlessly*, wrapped around the needs and preferences of the individual, so that it makes no difference who is providing individual services.
- *Measuring the health and wellbeing outcomes which matter to people*, and using that information to support improvement and better collaborative decision-making.
- *Proactively supporting people* throughout the whole of their lives, and through the whole of Wales, making an extra effort to reach those most in need to help reduce the health and wellbeing inequalities that exist.
- *Driving transformative change* through strong leadership and clear decision-making, adopting good practice and new models nationally, more open and confident engagement with external partners.
- *Promoting the distinctive values and culture* of the Welsh whole system approach with pride, making the case for how different choices are delivering more equitable outcomes and making Wales a better place in which to live and work.

The Plan is open-ended and thus not rigidly fixed, noting that there are too many different services, delivered over such a wide range of settings which would evolve in ways not entirely or exactly predictable. There is an emphasis on the sharing of learning because it makes no sense at all for every locality cluster to design a model of care from scratch if there are already good practices recognised elsewhere in Wales, in other parts of the UK or even internationally.

Among the actions in the Plan are:

- Regional Partnership Boards (RPBs) to drive the development of seamless health and social care local partnership models, working in tandem with local clusters.
- A major review of the existing programme boards, networks, delivery mechanisms, funds and other initiatives, with consideration being given to align and merge this landscape with a national Transformation Programme.
- A £100 million time-limited Transformation Fund targeted towards the rapid development of new models of health and social care, selected with the potential to scale up to a wider population base and aligned with national priorities.

- Ensuring that planning and governance systems are aligned, as far as is possible, across health and social care services in order to remove any barriers to delivery of new models of care.
- Recognition of greater parity of esteem between health and social care professionals and support for the vital role played by the informal workforce of unpaid carers and volunteers.

Leadership development

The Plan asserts that the best new care models all share a common characteristic – a broad multidisciplinary team approach where well-trained people work together effectively with all the up-to-date information about an individual's circumstances and preferences. Accordingly, the Plan proposes:

- That Health Education and Improvement Wales (HEIW) and Social Care Wales (SCW) be commissioned to jointly develop a long-term workforce strategy in partnership with the NHS, local government, the voluntary and independent sectors, as well as regulators, professional bodies and education providers.
- All health and social care organisations will need to establish their own strategic partnerships with education providers across Wales.
- A small number of Intensive Learning Academies will be established, focused on the professional capability needed for the future. These will act as hubs for developing the skills and expertise needed, for sharing knowledge and good practice, for translating research into outcomes and for working with external partners. Graduates of the academies can then take a leading role in supporting the redesign of the system/policy in key areas and act as informed advocates of change.
- A new leadership development competency framework and associated development programmes will be developed. This is likely to involve a focus on leadership in locality GP clusters and in the leadership of Regional Partnership Boards.
- Much of the delivery of programmes and activity is likely to be delivered by Academi Wales – the centre of excellence in leadership and management development for the public services in Wales.

England

Context

It was noted in 2017 that nearly 20 years of initiatives had not yet led to system-wide integrated services, and what had occurred so far was largely top-down and primarily concerned with organisations, budgets and processes. Shifts in policy emphasis and the reorganisations promoting competition within the NHS had complicated the path towards health and social care integration (Beveridge et al., 2017).

The NHS England *Five Year Forward View (FYFV)* of 2014 led to experimenta-tion with new care models (called Vanguards) at 50 sites in 2015. These comprised *Primary and Acute Care systems (PACs)* – where hospitals took the lead in joining up acute health services with General Practitioner, community, mental health and local authority social services, and *Multi-specialty Community Providers (MCPs)* involving GPs working to scale to forge greater links with community, mental health and social services. Each model sought to integrate care and improve population health, focusing on places and populations, rather than organisations. The Vanguard sites that made the most progress demonstrated qualities such as strong leadership, trusting relationships, co-operative behaviours and a collective willingness to work together to address system-wide problems. In parallel, work was initiated on the development of *Sustainability and Transformation Plans (STPs,* later relabelled *Partnerships)*. These ten sites were intended to supplement, rather than replace the accountabilities of existing organisations, and aimed to integrate care and transform services. An STP Board, headed by a chair or leader would have appropriate programme support and the precise way that it worked would vary according to local needs. The learning from the Vanguard sites has been expanded and upgraded to the ten STPs.

Each of the STP sites demonstrates different strengths and weaknesses and this variable maturity means that there is not a binary distinction between STPs and the development of ICPs, ICSs and ACOs. An evolutionary future approach is envisaged, with the potential developments including:

- *Integrated Care Partnerships (ICPs):* Alliances of local NHS providers working together to deliver care by agreeing to collaborate, rather than compete. They would involve hospitals, community services, mental health services and GPs. Social care and the third and private sectors might also be involved. ICPs typically involve PACs and MCPs and the boundaries between these two entities are increasingly being blurred.
- *Integrated Care Systems (previously Accountable Care Systems) (ICSs):* These bring together NHS providers and commissioners with local authorities to work in partnership to improve health and social care within their area. They have no statutory basis but rest upon the willingness of the constituent organisations to work successfully together. They hold the accountability for care across an identified local system and the organisations in the system take a collective role in the provision of health (and possibly social) care. They are expected to take the lead in planning and commissioning care for their populations and in providing systems leadership. The intention is that all STPs will become ICSs, while some may develop to become ACOs.
- *Accountable Care Organisations (ACOs):* These are established when commis-sioners award a long-term contract to a single organisation to provide a range of health and social care services to a defined population following a process of competitive procurement. It involves a formalising of previous partnership agreements and potentially involves a bigger role for the private sector.

An STP Delivery Unit was established in 2017 as a joint programme between NHS England and NHS Improvement in order to ensure that STPs were supported through a bespoke system-level diagnosis and high-impact plan for targeted support and interventions.

Leadership development

The NHS Leadership Academy for England has developed a *Systems Leadership Development Framework (SLDF)* (NHS Leadership Academy, 2016) which comprises four interconnecting domains. These are:

- *Individual Effectiveness:* This focuses on the effectiveness and resilience of the individual system leader and their role in both their organisation and the system as a whole. It aims to develop new behaviours and ways of working that promote a collaborative approach.
- *Relationships and Connectivity:* This involves creating the right kind of relationships with communities and partners; people coming together for a purpose; place-based or pathway-led services and aiming to develop a consistency of approach or to tackle complex issues collectively.
- *Innovations and Improvement:* This addresses creating new ways of thinking, experimentation and discovery and the application of improvement methodologies, testing and learning, spreading and adopting better ways of doing things.
- *Learning and Capacity-Building:* This comprises the creation of a learning system and a culture of transparency and sharing, enabling the awareness of best practice and the development of common understanding. Being inclusive and seeking contributions from all the stakeholders involved, including citizens and communities. Building diverse teams and inclusive cultures to enable greater understanding.

Each of these domains is populated by a number of specific behavioural descriptors which need to be demonstrated in order to create the leadership climate and culture that lays the foundation for transformation across networks of organisations and health and social care systems.

Working through the Leadership Academy's *Local Development Partners (LDPs)*, i. e. local 'regional' leadership academies, the expectation is that the LDPs adopt a consultancy approach and use the Framework to work with identified geographical areas within their local STP patch in order to identify their local needs and priorities and to craft a variety of interventions to best meet the leadership and system development needs which are identified. These interventions are 'bespoke' and vary depending upon need and priorities.

A 'menu' of interventions (effectively a mix of leader and leadership approaches) is offered, based upon the four domains of the SLDF. They comprise:

Individual Effectiveness: Leadership development programmes; coaching and mentoring; developing inclusive mind sets and behaviours; skills development workshops;

shadowing; buddying; exposure to different roles and environments; individual diagnostics.

Relationships and Connectivity: Facilitated group conversations; action learning sets; team and group coaching; holding courageous conversations; conferences and masterclasses; supporting network development; team and group diagnostics.

Innovations and Improvement: Leading complex change; developing and leading agile and lean services; quality improvement skills; innovation through thinking differently.

Learning and Capacity-Building: Talent development approaches and interventions; developing diverse community engagement/social movements; systems thinking and collective leadership; effective knowledge sharing.

References

Audit Scotland (2015) *Health and Social Care Integration*, Edinburgh: Audit Scotland

Beveridge, J., Burkett, M., Owens-Nash, G., Quick, H., Whittingham, A. & McDougall, A. (2017) *Health and Social Care Integration*, London: National Audit Office

Dayan, M. & Edwards, N. (2017) *Learning from Scotland's NHS*, London: Nuffield Trust

Department of Health (2016a) *Health and Wellbeing 2026: Delivering Together*, Belfast: Department of Health, Northern Ireland

Department of Health (2016b) *Systems, Not Structures: Changing Health and Social Care: Expert Panel Report*, Belfast: Department of Health, Northern Ireland

Department of Health (2017) *HSC Collective Leadership Strategy*, Belfast: Department of Health, Northern Ireland

Donaldson, L., Rutter, P. & Henderson, M. (2014) *The Right Time, the Right Place: An Expert Examination of the Application of Health and Social Care Governance Arrangements for Ensuring the Quality of Care Provision in Northern Ireland*, Belfast: Department of Health, Northern Ireland

Ham, C., Heenan, D., Longley, M. & Steel, D. (2013) *Integrated Care in Northern Ireland, Scotland and Wales: Lessons for England*, London: Kings Fund

NHS Leadership Academy (2016) *Developing Systems Leadership: Interventions, Options and Opportunities*, Leeds: NHS Leadership Academy

Sharp, C. (2018) *Learning and Outcomes from Leadership for Integration: Final Report*, Edinburgh: Research for Real for NHS Education for Scotland/ Scottish Social Services Council/ Royal College of General Practitioners (Scotland)

Welsh Assembly (2018) *A Revolution from Within: Transforming Health and Care in Wales: The Parliamentary Review of Health and Social Care in Wales: Final Report*, Cardiff: Welsh Assembly

Welsh Government (2018) *A Healthier Wales: Our Plan for Health and Social Care*, Cardiff: Welsh Government

7

VIGNETTES AND PERSONAL ACCOUNTS

This chapter alternates a series of 'vignettes', or external descriptions of work on developing integrated care and systems leadership in a variety of locations, with personal accounts of both individuals and groups – a series of 'inside' viewpoints.

The Millom experience (Howarth et al., 2017)

In 2014 the North West England NHS Leadership Academy offered its member organisations the opportunity to bid for a systems leadership grant of up to £20,000. The Cumbria Learning and Improvement Collaborative (CLIC) is a shared 'umbrella' initiative made up of health care, social care and third sector providers in the Cumbria and the Morecambe Bay area and this grouping together with the Millom Alliance submitted a joint bid to develop an 'out of hospital' leadership programme which was intended to develop the skills needed for collective leadership and so to develop health, public sector and community leaders together to lead change for the population of Millom.

The outcomes of the leadership programme included:

- Increased knowledge and capability of leaders within the out-of-hospital system.
- More impactful working relationships between leaders within primary care communities.
- Enhanced performance in out-of-hospital care through effective leadership based on clarity of shared purpose, effective systems and planning of service change with clear measures of the impact of change on the health care system.

The key outputs comprised:

- An innovative programme that supported systems leadership capability of a range of formal and informal leaders within communities in Cumbria.
- A written evaluation of the pilot development programme.
- Three leadership coaches competent and confident to deliver future programmes.
- A knowledge hub/portal for easy access to information on systems leadership to support self-development.

The longer-term benefits to the health and social care system are:

- Better quality care for less.
- Reduced costs for commissioners.
- Reduced deficits for providers.
- Support and sustainability for General Practice.
- A stronger primary and community team working 7/7 supported by specialists using technology.
- Closer working between specialists and community and primary care, delivering the clinical model and the clinical pathways required in order to radically reduce pressure and flow to the acute hospitals.

Mature conversations and practical actions (Sharp, 2018)

One of the Collaborative Leadership In Practice (CLIP) sites in North Lanarkshire is a large group of about 20 people that includes health and social care managers for localities, clinical leads from health, cluster quality leads and GPs. This group had been meeting for several months and there has been good continuity of attendance.

This is, at least in part, because there is financial provision for GPs to fund a locum or other arrangement whilst they attend meetings. One comment was that 'the first meetings were all about the money, about how to release GPs to be there', but it was clear by a later stage that this protected time was valued and had real and practical consequences.

On one occasion the meeting starts with people sharing what is on their minds. Lots of comments are about wanting to hear about what is happening and having a chance to talk to each other. Some talk of wanting to move things on and get support or money from other people in the room. If there is a common thread, it might be that 'we can lift our eyes off the immediate future and start to think about the longer term'. Another is their common interest in finding ways to put 'realistic medicine' into practice, so that the person receiving health and social care is at the centre of decision-making and has a personalised approach to their care.

There are six localities represented and each has an 'experiment' – something that they are in the process of testing-out. These relate to how GPs and other parts of health and social care can support each other for the benefit of patients and communities. For example, one is setting up a clinical forum; another is looking at home support and a third at prescribing practices and homecare costs. The latter example is up for an award; it arose from an initial desire to reduce costs of home care due to the need for a prompt to a patient to take medication. Through discussion the group learned that GPs did not know who was getting home support. They describe this as

> exactly this kind of problem solving that we're needing. People went over and above the norm and worked together making a real effort to change things, including the GPs, home care and pharmacy support. There were lots of good ideas … some really simple things, like different types of statins can be taken at different times of the day, checking whether people are actually taking their medication and not storing it in their cupboards. It couldn't have been done when we had two separate organisations.

Another expresses their view about the value of this kind of process – 'It's refreshing to have a breadth of views when looking at problems and it's more person-centred.'

In making this kind of progress there is history to contend with. Some GPs have been isolated, perhaps working on their own and not necessarily seeking to influence the wider health and social care system. For the future, there is an impending change of contract for GPs and a general anxiety about having to do more with less funding. In the midst of all this, operational managers are trying to work out how decisions that, on the face of it, may seem operational, but do impact on GP functions. They want to help the GPs – they are full of questions and are also acutely aware of professional boundaries – 'the sensitivities might prevent us from having a conversation about something that we do need to talk about – how can we help you out as GPs?' For themselves, the GPs are exploring how to be better influencers, working out how they best fit into what is happening in localities and wondering 'How do we share information when we can't be at everything?' and 'How do we best support carers who are anxious about being left alone to care and fearing that they will not be able to get back into the system when they need it?'

There is a lot of sharing of practical information, which may go some way to make up for the inevitable oversight, given workloads and schedules – 'It's very easy to miss written information that's shared when it's embedded in a whole lot of papers for a meeting that I'm not attending.'

In a plenary session they talk about how they are seeing 'An increasingly collective ethos forming'. They are asking questions of each other about what decisions might be made collectively – 'What do we have authority to make decisions about?' 'Are we actually allowed to do these things?' Someone makes a joke about mixed messages – 'We'll get reprimanded if it goes out of line – or we might get an award if it goes well!'

At times there is frustration and genuine annoyance amongst the group. Some of them say that this is about the slow pace of change and the degree of fragility within General Practice. However, there is a benefit to the degree of honesty in the room – 'Through CLIP I have come to appreciate and have a better understanding of the conditions under which other people are working – which makes it less frustrating for me.'

Prevention of chronic diseases (Richardson et al., 2016)

The London Borough of Tower Hamlets has a population with high levels of deprivation and historically poor outcomes, a simple commissioning footprint for care outside the hospital, but a complicated acute health care landscape with a huge provider hospital facing very large financial pressures and multiple Clinical Commissioning Groups (CCGs) that need to be involved to address it. Primary care had, for many years, struggled to meet local population needs. Its integrated care programme focused on integration driven through primary care transformation.

A network of GP practices was set up aligned with other providers, so facilitating the coming together of GP practices to form networks that became organisational, rather than simply meetings. This was supported by a significant organisation development programme at the outset and the investment of substantial resources in recruiting and training the workforce.

The initial focus was on 11,000 diabetic patients (4% of the population), then expanded quickly to cover 20% of the population with chronic conditions. The programme had an initial focus on primary care transformation and this extended to a wider range of interventions involving public health, community and mental health and social care across chronic and complex conditions.

The Borough has a young and mixed ethnic population, with over 30% of the population Bangladeshi, a high burden of chronic disease and a complicated provider environment with poor primary care provision and access. Primary care had made significant improvements driven by a culture and ambition to do more. The focus was primarily on health and social care coordination via primary care to improve prevention and early intervention. To do this specific packages of care were designed for a range of chronic conditions.

These care packages set out the key interactions that each patient required during a year of care, i.e. the type, number and duration of appointments and the workforce needed to provide them. A care model was designed with enhanced levels of care being delivered by new staff who connected GP practice staff with community and hospital staff.

A detailed information sharing system has been created that allows robust performance tracking that has been directly linked to payment on a quarterly basis. A new payment model was developed that was fundamental to the success of the wider programme. The funding for care packages was provided at a GP network level, with networks able to decide how and where to spend their funding. Seventy per cent of the budget was provided up-front, with 30% provided in return for reaching care package targets. Networks were allowed to use these funds autonomously to achieve the key performance indicator (KPI) targets, and as a result, could decide to apply them to particular areas of need if they wished. This allowed the networks to innovate and handle resources from a front-line perspective, as well as incentivising outcomes. Since the creation of the Tower Hamlets Clinical Commissioning Group the performance element of the contract has come under renegotiation. Some care packages have been re-arranged from a 70/30 split to a 60/40 split, with a heavier weighting on the target-based funding. Local authority providers have also asked for a 30/70 split, meaning most of the money would be based on outcomes. As well as renegotiating the contract, the CCG is looking for further means to align incentives, payments and providers, offering to share Quality, Innovation, Productivity and Prevention (QIPP) money if providers and the CCG can reduce non-elective activity.

It has been consistently noted that changing the flow of money is essential to provide for changes in the patterns of resources and care delivered.

One for all and all for one (Sharp, 2018)

'We are aiming to create a co-operative and friendly integrated team who work with people to provide fantastic care. We call this work "All for one and one for all".' It's a great ambition for Annan in Dumfries and Galloway. Annan is unusual as the Health and Social Care Partnership (HSCP) have used Integrated Care Fund money to develop the 'one team' approach across the localities. The project manager says:

> If I'd used the term CLIP in the initial invites to people they would have seen it and thought 'That's not for me' – I would have just got the senior managers. 'Collaborative Leadership in Practice' is too big and scary and would put people off. So an early step was to come up with our own term, that was meaningful for us. That was a painful process too as we swapped emails and said what we liked or didn't like. We were discussing it at a management team meeting when someone said 'It sounds like The Three Musketeers', so 'One for all and all for one' has become our way of describing what we're about.

The management team had been developing a set of principles that we wanted the one team to work to. These were drawing on the Buurtzorg model, a Dutch model of community care being tested in Scotland (Brindle, 2017). They were interested in what they thought might work locally, not as a directive for what people should do, but to provide a framework to help practitioners develop their ideas and creative responses to issues. The first CLIP session was a chance to have external facilitation of the process to develop their own sense of what those principles might mean to them.

The CLIP facilitator ran an Open Space event. Lots of people in the room had not experienced this before. The project manager comments:

When I pitch up people know me, so it was helpful to have an 'outsider' there. It detaches us a bit from our normality. In this area most people have worked with each other for years and whilst that can be a strength, we might sometimes feel we know each other too well! The fact that people did not know the facilitator and he had no legacy in the area was a positive.

The day was good.

The event attracted a fantastic mix of people. There was no part of health and social care that wasn't represented and people were able to suggest topics and choose which conversation they wanted to join. That enabled us to come up with some really great ideas that people engaged with and mostly continue to engage with. Of course, some of the conversations on that day went nowhere. Somebody offered to host a conversation about 'How do we stop our patients being so demanding?' That attracted the biggest number of people – people were interested in whether it was possible to have patient participation groups around a GP practice. Nurses were interested in how to work with patients' relatives in a hospital setting and GPs were concerned with patients that keep coming back many times. This was a big topic about engagement and empowerment which didn't progress much, probably because it was too big.

There were positive comments in the feedback after the event – 'The open space was really positive – any idea was given a chance.' People liked the fact that it brought different professionals into the room to discuss issues and find common ground. They enjoyed hearing other perspectives and finding some simple actions that might make a difference.

The project manager was surprised at the breadth of people's ideas and the fearlessness of them.

They didn't pick the easy things – they went for the ones that were important for them. I thought some of the issues might be too complicated and difficult, but where things have got off the ground since then, they have gone well and some of the conversations that started as part of the Open Space are still going on all these months later. For example, the mental health team are having some really good discussions and the person-centred team have been looking at power of attorney and have been working with local solicitors to ensure there is a consistent approach in Annan, looking at local events around planning for the future for both staff and public. One of the senior district nurses was disappointed that her wish to see insulin injections administered by carers in care homes came up against several barriers, but she is tenacious and is now looking at getting third year student nurses in care homes to train care home staff on specific topics. These are small steps – but signal a change in approach.

The project manager concludes:

> The biggest thing is to get people to share their ideas, and to know that they are 'allowed' to do that. They might think that they don't have the capacity to do this or that someone needs to tell them what to do. Or simply that it's not been the way we do things round here. Now I'm pleased to see that there are lots of fantastic developments. They're all very collaborative and all coming from the folk on the ground. Whether you call it collaborative leadership or not, it seems to be working.

Greater Manchester devolution (Holbourn & Westwood, 2017)

In February, 2015 systems leaders in Manchester were among 37 NHS organisations and local authorities that signed the Greater Manchester devolution agreement with the UK Government which would enable them to take control of health and social care spending and decision-making in the region. This became effective on 1 April 2016 and set out a vision across Greater Manchester. A review conducted in 2017 concluded that:

- Systems leaders and political leaders in Greater Manchester had a clear, credible and compelling strategy and vision of future health and social care services and that there was a sense of a true partnership between those services based on a significant period of building relationships across health and social care and voluntary, community and social enterprise agencies. This vision was clearly communicated and understood at all levels of health and social care commissioning organisations, secondary care providers, voluntary sector organisations and social care providers.
- There was good buy-in to the Greater Manchester vision from local political leaders through to frontline health and social care staff. Staff were engaged and enthusiastic about the long-term strategic vision for Greater Manchester and saw integrated working as a way to improve services for people, to enhance their own working arrangements and as a force for positive change.
- A powerful guiding coalition was creating the conditions for integration of services.
- In April, 2017 formal arrangements were established for integrating the commissioning of services across health and social care by the creation of Manchester Health and Care Commissioning (MHCC). This is a single commissioning voice, underpinned by shared governance and a single financial budget for the local authority and Clinical Commissioning Group to improve the population's health and wellbeing.
- A single hospital provider – the Manchester University NHS Foundation Trust was created in October, 2017 through the merger of previous NHS Trusts.
- A Local Care Organisation (LCO) became operational from April, 2018 and brought together in a collaborative partnership mental health services, community services, General Practitioners and social services working in

multi-professional teams. Within the LCO 12 neighbourhood boards are being developed so that priorities and neighbourhood plans can be developed around local community identities.

• Where services were co-located or integrated, staff reported that relationships between professionals were good, with improved communication and information-sharing.

• There was a recognition that the long-term programme of change would inevitably take time.

Commitment and perseverance pays off (Sharp, 2018)

Kilmacolm is a small community outwith the three main towns in Inverclyde. Its semi-rural location makes it both similar and different to the rest of Inverclyde and it is perceived as a comparatively affluent community.

The CLIP programme worked with a small and committed multi-disciplinary group of two General Practitioners, a lead Allied Health Professions (AHP) manager, nurses, practice managers and a manager from the Health and Social Care Partnership. They first met in December, 2016 and were keen to address community needs, particularly for a vulnerable group of frail elderly (almost) housebound people. This was seen as both a medical and a social issue; social isolation and loneliness sometimes meant that people were booking multiple GP appointments they did not really need. Early discussions suggested that despite there seeming to be a number of clubs and activities happening, they were not sure how well used they were or whether the difficulty was a lack of public transport.

In the early days, some of the group said that they would leave meetings full of enthusiasm, and later reflect and agree they needed to take a different approach:

> We may have jumped in too deep with big ideas without assessing the wishes or needs of the community. I think we are good at thinking what we think the community needs, but I'm not sure how we tally that up with actual hard data or patient needs from the community.

As a CLIP group, they agreed a dual focus, exploring how they could work better together and how they might influence the community infrastructure in Kilmacolm. Initially, work to look at areas that overlap or cause problems in the pathways between the GPs and the AHP services took up a lot of the effort. Their success in clarifying referral options through a single point of access gave the group confidence that they could indeed connect and work together to effect change on a wider basis, by looking at what they might achieve for the socially isolated members of the community.

Tackling this brought its own frustrations. They were not able to get the local third sector involved at first, due to staffing and financial issues, although they did learn that the Community Connectors pilot project in Inverclyde had found it difficult to get the local population engaged.

It was important to the group that they could have real confidence in any new directory of community services. The momentum was impressive. A lot of activity went on between meetings, with the group members researching what resources existed locally and finding inspiring examples of directories from further afield. Amongst other things, they made some new discoveries and connections – they found a book club service to the housebound that they didn't know about; got an engaging response from the local school to the idea of pupils supporting the work as part of an IT-based Duke of Edinburgh award and made contact with the Reaching Older Adults (ROAR) group in nearby Renfrewshire, in the hope that they might be able to expand their offer into the area.

In September-October, 2017, they conducted a survey at one of the GP practices, achieving over 80 replies. Unintentionally, this gave them some useful feedback about the services from the surgery. At the same time, more than half of the people responding did have ideas for services in the local community and commented on what services they would use if they were available. It showed that people did not necessarily know about what already existed and that the ideas that the professionals had were not far off the mark. Although a few people wanted to see better transport, a bigger theme was a desire to keep fit, active and mobile. Having the data in this way gave the group the confidence they needed to take ideas forward.

Their efforts have helped them to get more recognition of the community of Kilmacolm in the wider HSCP – 'Inverclyde is assumed to be a small place where you're never more than two minutes from Greenock town centre … people haven't necessarily thought about how the design of our services affects a small but distinct community like Kilmacolm.' Their efforts are paying off and they have a strong expectation that people will gain from having better information about services that can impact on their quality of life. They have seen this work as an opportunity to shape the care that is provided locally. The two GP practices have benefited both from their new knowledge of what is available in the community and from the practical partnership working amongst local health and social care professionals, as they have raised their confidence and trust in one another. They are hopeful that a new mind-set takes root, that sees their geography as an asset, rather than a problem.

Although the work is still very much in progress, there has been a great deal of learning. One of the GPs says 'There has been a lot of enthusiasm to make things better amongst us. We cannot underestimate how much we learn through involving other teams and communicating better. We've learned a lot about different agencies.' The other GP acknowledges that there is still quite a long way to go but says 'We have to remember where we were! I feel we've gone a long way. We have demonstrated that we have ambitions, that we have a voice for Kilmacolm and that's quite a big deal. We speak to each other!'

There is also learning about the bigger picture and the roles of others. 'I also learned that the scope of the HSCP is huge. It's much bigger than I had realised. I have a better understanding of how all the cogs are turning and of the sheer scale of other people's roles.' There is more confidence that the locality is 'on the radar' and a better understanding that while people in Kilmacolm may be 'asset-rich' they are often 'relationship-poor' – they are lonely.

Their commitment and perseverance are paying off. They are positive about the value of the time spent. 'This work shows it is good to take more time to think.' At the same time there is a shared anxiety that it might become 'one of those things that's allowed to drop'. At the final CLIP session, they were still wondering if they have all the right people around the table and who else they need to involve to keep up their momentum.

The long journey (Richardson et al., 2016)

Northumberland has been pursuing integration of health and social care services since the late 1990s, with many of the local systems leaders being involved in this for a significant part of the journey. The area is marked with an older population with poor health, but there is separation of the commissioning and provider functions with clear Clinical Commissioning Group (CCG)/local authority alignment and a strong provider in the Northumbria Healthcare Foundation NHS Trust. Community and mental health services have been integrated into a previously acute Trust and a community care business unit has been set up, within which social care is linked to community and secondary care. A General Practitioner sits as the Medical Director of the Trust. Locality Integrated Networks (LINs) have been created built on risk-sharing mechanisms between the CCG, local authorities and care providers. These began with community and acute healthcare integration and then brought in nursing homes and primary care. The health and social care workforce has been re-oriented to structure them around Multi-Disciplinary Teams (MDTs).

An early focus was on the frail elderly with a high risk of Accident and Emergency and hospital admission. A Northumbria Frail Elderly Pathway was devised to improve care for the very high-risk frail elderly and to reduce the emergency admissions attributed to them. Patients were identified in primary, secondary and community care services and referred to the Pathway, while subsequently being added to a high-risk register. Patients on the register were targeted for assessment by nurses and GPs, reviewed by a Multi-Disciplinary Team (MDT) and had care packages identified and put in place for them. This provided a coordinated care pathway structured round the needs of high-risk patients, seeking to identify such people before an Accident and Emergency attendance or a hospital admission and thus provided packages of care outside the hospital. The register keeps these people on the radar of primary care, social care and psychiatric care and ensures that they are provided with daily social care. This exercise drew on a diverse range of funding streams and achieved reductions of some 36% in emergency admissions.

System-wide commitment has been secured, together with investment of £8.3 million to deliver an Integrated Primary and Acute Care System (IPACS), joining-up GP, hospital, community and mental health services with social care and cutting across organisational barriers, delivering shared information management systems and bringing together commissioning responsibility for the whole health and social care economy.

References

Brindle, D. (2017) Buurtzog: The Dutch Model of Neighbourhood Care that Is Going Global, *The Guardian*, 9 May

Holbourn, A. & Westwood, D. (2017) *Manchester: Local System Review Report: Health and Wellbeing Board*, London: Care Quality Commission

Howarth, J., Davis, D., Worsley-Cox, K., Brumby, J. & Fleming, R. (2017) Citizen-Led Healthcare: Learning from the Millom Experience, *International Journal of Integrated Care*, 17(5)

Richardson, B., Carnall, S., Gault, W. & Coleridge, A. (2016) *The Journey to Integration: Learning from Seven Leading Localities*, London: Carnall Farrar for Local Government Association

Sharp, C. (2018) *Learning and Outcomes from Leadership for Integration: Final Report*, Edinburgh: Research for Real for NHS Education for Scotland/Scottish Social Services Council/Royal College of General Practitioners (Scotland)

8

LESSONS LEARNED

This chapter seeks to identify the major lessons learned from the development of systems leadership across all the four parts of the UK.

If systems leadership for the integration of health and social care is recognised to be a work in progress, what are the key lessons that have been learned so far (Ham et al., 2013; Ham, 2018)?

- There needs to be in place a sustained and **long-term commitment** to the fostering of integrated care and to systems leadership as a policy priority for the governments in all the parts of the UK. This commitment needs to be maintained and sustained over a sufficiently long period of time in order to enable real positive impacts to be made and then demonstrated. It should therefore not be subject to interruptive short-term policy switches and variations.
- It needs to be recognised that this long-term commitment to developing integrated care and systems leadership **takes both time and energy**, while those concerned also having to deal with the continuing day-to-day operational pressures which face health and social care. The danger is always that the urgent tends to drive out the important, but the challenges involved will never be met by existing and future systems leaders simply trying to work harder or faster – new and different ways of working are absolutely necessary.
- Every effort needs to be made to ensure that working towards integrated care through systems leadership is **a true marriage of equal partners** between health and social care and between statutory, private and third sector agencies. This highlights the importance of the NHS in particular engaging more fully with local authorities and with other partners, and so avoiding an NHS-only view of the world taking precedence. Likewise, local government and private and third sector organisations need to engage more creatively with the NHS at all levels.

- **Appropriate governance arrangements** need to be devised locally that enable health and social care organisations to work together in order to develop their joint strategies and actions. Such local governance arrangements need to encompass existing community, political, clinical and professional leadership. Where there is a 'cluttered landscape' of different and potentially overlapping bodies (and hence often a series of confused or diffuse responsibilities), these will need to be clarified and/or simplified. The danger is that such unclear purpose and function can lead to longer and longer agendas and to interminable formal meetings. This may mean putting into place governance arrangements such as memoranda of understanding and partnership boards that enable progress to be made within existing statutory frameworks. This can enable the real work to succeed. It is not enough, however, just to be a 'coalition of the willing' involving a few isolated supporters – it is vital that every part of the local system is ultimately engaged. Rather than a main focus on continuing changes to organisational structures, the myriad barriers to integrated care which exist also need to be addressed. The impetus for such development needs to be increasingly emergent, flexible and 'organic', rather than legal or structural, with form gradually following function.
- Coherent **national policies to promote and support systems leadership** need to be put in place – especially integrated performance frameworks and single outcomes frameworks. Performance management in particular needs to move from short-term towards longer-term approaches. Likewise, **common IT platforms** need to be developed.
- **Involving people who use services** and, where appropriate, their carers is essential to the design, implementation and sustainability of services that really meet the needs of the people who use them.
- Systems leaders will need to **beware of the temptation to turn wicked problems into tame problems**, or to assume that wicked problems can simply be solved by the adoption of tame problem tools and techniques. Typically, this assumption involves segmenting the issue and setting up project groups who find that they cannot solve the problems – so the issues concerned continue to go round and round.
- As far as humanly possible there needs to be **continuing organisational and staffing stability** to avoid the many distractions and delays that occur when organisational structures are altered frequently and key staff move on or are replaced. Where the success of systems leadership depends largely upon an individual or group of individuals, if the initiative stays with them, the danger is that it will potentially also leave with them. The challenge is to balance stability of leadership (which is crucial for maintaining momentum) with the need to build outwards to a broader coalition of leaders (which risks diluting that momentum).
- There needs to be a recognition that effective working relationships are the major key to success and so the development of systems leadership at all levels and in all stakeholder organisations has to be clearly and consistently supported. Local leaders therefore need to invest significant time and effort in the

building of trust and collaborative relationships and in overcoming organisational protectionism, competitive behaviours and those poor relationships which have, in the past, created and maintained barriers to integrated working.

- Collaborative interpersonal or social skills are now essential to the success of systems leadership, through the creation and sustaining of healthy working relationships. Therefore, partner organisations need to **make the ability to collaborate a key requirement** for their recruitment, selection, promotion and development at every level. This clearly has major implications for talent management programmes in statutory health and social care organisations.
- **Co-locating teams**, creating shared spaces in which individuals can step outside their professional and managerial silos, together with **brokering secondments, attachments and shadowing**, can all help to physically bring people together and thus to overcome entrenched organisational, cultural and professional barriers.
- There needs to be a willingness to provide both the **financial and education and training support and flexibilities** needed to enable the introduction of new models of care. **Better-aligned financial incentives** need to be developed and **inter-professional education and training** at undergraduate, post-graduate and continuing professional development levels especially need to be strengthened.
- There has to be a willingness on the part of systems leaders to understand and respect where appropriate, but also to challenge and overcome where necessary, the existing **professional, cultural and behavioural barriers** between health and social care. As has often been said, the danger is that 'culture eats strategy for breakfast'.
- Priority needs to be given to **investment in evaluation** in order to assess the impact of integrated care and of systems leadership. Thus, learning from local initiatives needs to be captured and shared on a continuing basis so that integrated care and systems leadership become increasingly evidence-based.
- **National regulators** need to change their ways of working in order to support integration and systems leadership. Any reversion to top-down performance management will certainly stymie this. The danger is that when the going gets tough the NHS tends to simply revert to this variety of performance management and local authorities to an insistence on the primacy of local differences.
- **Joint health and social care inspections** need to increasingly be the norm.
- While traditionally the development of leaders in health and social care has been undertaken on an individual basis through leader development programmes, increasingly the emphasis needs to turn towards **leadership development, featuring whole multi-agency and multi-professional teams and involving innovative designs.**
- Each of the parts of the UK have important differences in their health and social care arrangements and their approaches to systems leadership obviously reflect these. There is, however, in existence something of a 'not invented

here' orientation, both within and between the constituent parts of the UK and internationally, and so the scope for learning from the valuable experience of a different system may quite easily be lost. A recent review of the arrangements across the UK (conducted for the NHS alone) stated that 'a lack of willingness to learn from each other may deprive the four NHSs of a unique opportunity to develop positive change for the NHS as a whole' (Doherty, 2015). That applies not just within the four NHSs, but right across the health and social care spectrum in all four parts of the UK. Although variation is obviously crucial in ensuring that local services meet and serve local needs, not learning from what has been tried before, or tried elsewhere, is costly, time-intensive and risks duplicating the progress that has been made in other places. **Sharing and learning from the experience of others needs to be accelerated** because it is not sensible to continuously keep on reinventing the wheel. The goal should be to 'steal, adapt and plagiarise with pride'!

References

Doherty, S. (2015) *The Organisation of the NHS in the UK: Comparing Structures in the Four Countries*, Cardiff: National Assembly for Wales Research Paper

Ham, C. (2018) *Making Sense of Integrated Care Systems, Integrated Care Partnerships and Accountable Care Organisations in the NHS in England*, London: Kings Fund

Ham, C., Heenan, D., Longley, M. & Steel, D. (2013) *Integrated Care in Northern Ireland, Scotland and Wales: Lessons for England*, London: Kings Fund

9

AND FINALLY ...

The change of metaphor from machine to living system has profound consequences for health and social care, both locally and nationally, in all parts of the UK. Unlearning the previous conventional ways of seeing, thinking and acting can be both a disturbing and uncomfortable process. However, the potential beneficial outcomes for individuals, families and communities are enormous. It is important to remember that:

> Self-organising, non-linear systems are inherently unpredictable. They are not controllable. They are understandable only in the most general way. The goal of foreseeing the future exactly and preparing for it perfectly is unrealisable. The idea of making a complex system do just what you want it to do can be achieved only temporarily, at best. We can never fully understand our world, not in the way that reductionist science has led us to believe.
>
> Systems thinking leads to another conclusion, however – waiting, shining, obvious as soon as we stop being blinded by the illusion of control. It says there is plenty to do, of a different sort of 'doing'. The future can't be predicted, but it can be envisioned and brought lovingly into being. Systems can't be controlled, but they can be designed and redesigned. We can't surge forward with certainty into a world of no surprises, but we can expect surprises and learn from them, and even profit from them. We can't impose our will upon a system. We can listen to what the system tells us, and discover how its properties and our values can work together to bring forth something much better than could ever be produced by our will alone.
>
> *(Meadows, 2001)*

Reference

Meadows, D. (2001) Dancing with Systems, *Whole Earth*, 106: 58–63

FURTHER EXPLORATION AND READING

International Foundation for Integrated Care

The *International Foundation for Integrated Care* is a not-for-profit network that crosses organisational and professional boundaries in order to bring people together to advance the science, knowledge and adoption of integrated care policy and practice. It seeks to achieve this through the development and exchange of ideas among academics, researchers, managers, clinicians, policy makers and service users and carers throughout the world. Its goal is to provide a unique forum to bring these various perspectives together, with the ultimate aim of improving the experience of care for patients, their families and communities, while also improving the overall effectiveness of health and social care systems.

This is undertaken by:

- Publishing the latest integrated care related research, case studies and evidence in a peer-reviewed, open-access journal – the *International Journal for Integrated Care*. This is an online, open-access, peer-reviewed scientific journal that publishes original articles in the field of integrated care on a continuous basis. Further information is at www.ijic.org/
- Bringing people together to present and hear from the latest research, evidence, innovations and practice at international conferences.
- Developing both people and organisations by providing education and training support through an Integrated Care Academy.
- Undertaking primary research and providing research and evaluation support to integrated care research-based projects.
- Supporting a network of global members so that they might collaborate, share knowledge and ideas and discuss the latest ideas around integrated care.

Further information about the Foundation is obtainable at www.integratedca
refoundation.org

Journal of Integrated Care

The *Journal of Integrated Care* aims to facilitate the evidence-based integration of
health, social care and other community services to the benefit of service users,
patients and taxpayers. The target audience of the journal is managers and practitioners responsible for commissioning, planning and providing care services, as well
as academics studying or evaluating related policy. It publishes papers covering:

- UK and international policy and practice.
- The relationship between policy and practice (including both 'central/local'
  and 'bottom up/top down' perspectives).
- Outcomes and evaluation of practice, performance, quality and efficiency.
- Change management in relation to integrated care.
- Adult and children's services and their interface.
- Organisational/workforce development in the integrated care field.
- Multi-disciplinary and inter-agency approaches and partnerships between
  medicine, nursing, the allied health professions, social work and social care.
- The concerns of service users and carers.

Further information is available at www.emeraldinsight.com/journal/jica

Journal of Interprofessional Care

The *Journal of Interprofessional Care* disseminates research and new developments in the
field of interprofessional education and practice. The areas of practice covered by the
journal include primary, community and hospital care, health education and public
health and beyond health and social care into fields such as criminal justice and pri-
mary/elementary education.

More information is obtainable at www.tandfonline.com/toc/ijic20/current

International Centre for Integrated Care (IC4IC)

This Centre is based within the University of the West of Scotland and aims to
develop courageous and compassionate leaders and practitioners with the knowledge, skills and confidence to design, deliver and evaluate people-centred integrated care. It has four work-streams:

- *Leadership and Education* – Undergraduate, Masters-level and accreditable
  Continuing Professional Development (CPD).
- *Knowledge Exchange and Translation* – International webinars and special interest
  groups.

- *Action Research and Evaluation* – With a focus on frailty, dementia and personal outcomes.
- *System Coaching*

For further information contact:
Anne.hendry@lanarkshire.scot.nhs.uk
Mandy.andrew@lanarkshire.scot.nhs.uk
Helen.Rainey@uws.ac.uk

FURTHER READING

Systems: General

Capra, F. & Luisi, P. (2014) *The Systems View of Life: A Unifying Vision*, Cambridge: Cambridge University Press

Chapman, J. (2004) *System Failure: Why Governments Must Learn to Think Differently*, London: Demos

Edgren, L. & Barnard, K. (2012) Complex Adaptive Systems for Management of Integrated Care, *Leadership in Health Services*, 25(1): 39–51

Gordon, P., Plamping, D. & Pratt, J. (2010) *Working in Systems: The Landscapes Framework*, Leeds: Centre for Innovation in Health Management, University of Leeds

Kernick, D. (Ed.) (2004) *Complexity and Healthcare Organisation: A View from the Street*, Abingdon: Radcliffe Medical Press

Lewis, M. (2014) *High Performing Organisations: A Whole Systems Approach to Long Term Effectiveness*, Cardiff: Academi Wales

Malby, B. & Fischer, M. (2006) *Tools for Change: An Invitation to Dance*, Chichester: Kingsham Press

McMillan, E. (2008) *Complexity, Management and the Dynamics of Change*, Abingdon: Routledge

Meadows, D. & Wright, D. (Eds.) (2008) *Thinking in Systems: A Primer*, London: Chelsea Green Publishing

Oshry, B. (2007) *Seeing Systems: Unlocking the Mysteries of Organisational Life*, San Francisco: Berrett-Koehler

Pratt, J., Gordon, P. & Plamping, D. (2005) *Working Whole Systems: Putting Theory into Practice in Organisations*, Abingdon: Radcliffe Publishing

Sweeney, K. & Griffiths, S. (2002) *Complexity and Health Care*, Abingdon: Radcliffe Publishing

Integrated care: General

ADASS (2013) *Four Nations United: Critical Learning from Four Different Systems for the Successful Integration of Social Care and Health Services*, London: Association of Directors of Adult Social Services

Ball, R., Forbes, T., Parris, M. & Forsyth, L. (2010) The Evaluation of Partnership Working in the Delivery of Health and Social Care, *Public Policy & Administration*, 25(4): 387–407

Baxter, S., Johnson, M., Chambers, D., Sutton, A., Goyder, E. & Booth, A. (2018) The Effects of Integrated Care: A Systematic Review of UK and International Evidence, *BMC Health Services Research*, 18

Bohling-DaMetz, K. & Grundy, P. (2018) *Achieving the Provision of Integrated Care: Exploring the Development and Successful Implementation Internationally of New Models of Integrated Care*, London: National Association of Primary Care

Emerson, K., Nabatchi, T. & Balogh, S. (2012) An Integrated Framework for Collaborative Governance, *Journal of Public Administration Research & Theory*, 22(1): 1–29

Evans, D. & Forbes, T. (2009) Partnerships in Health and Social Care: England and Scotland Compared, *Public Policy & Adminstration*, 24(1): 67–83

Glasby, J. & Dickinson, H. (2014) *Partnership Working in Health and Social Care: What Is Integrated Care and How Can We Deliver It?*, 2nd edition, Bristol: Policy Press

Heenan, D. & Birrell, D. (2018) *The Integration of Health and Social Care in the UK*, London: Macmillan International

Hendry, A., Cariazo, A., Vanhecke, E. & Rodriguez-Laso, A. (2018) Integrated Care: A Collaborative Advantage for Frailty, *International Journal of Integrated Care*, 18(2)

Huxham, C. & Vangen, S. (2005) *Managing to Collaborate: The Theory and Practice of Collaborative Advantage*, Abingdon: Routledge

Kahane, A. (2004) *Solving Tough Problems: An Open Way of Talking, Listening and Creating New Realities*, San Francisco: Berrett-Koehler

Kahane, A. (2017) *Collaborating with the Enemy: How to Work with People You Don't Agree with, or Like, or Trust*, San Francisco: Berrett-Koehler

Kippin, H. & Fulford, B. (2016) *The Anatomy of Collaboration: A Resource for Leaders in Health, Social Care and Beyond*, London: Collaborate

Klinga, C., Hasson, H., Sachs, M. & Hansson, J. (2018) Understanding the Dynamics of Sustainable Change: A 20-Year Case Study of Integrated Health and Social Care, *BMC Health Services Research* 18: 400

Lloyd, J. & Wait, S. (2006) *Integrated Care: A Guide for Policymakers*, London: Alliance for Health and the Future

Martin, A. & Manley, K. (2017) Developing Standards for an Integrated Approach to Workplace Facilitation for Inter-Professional Teams in Health and Social Care Contexts: A Delphi Study, *Journal of Inter-Professional Care*, 32(1)

Maruthappa, M., Hasan, A. & Zeltner, T. (2015) Enablers and Barriers in Implementing Integrated Care, *Health Systems & Reform*, 1(4): 250–256

Mason, A., Goddard, M., Weatherley, H. & Chalkley, M. (2015) Integrating Funds for Health and Social Care: An Evidence Review, *Journal of Health Services Research & Policy*, 20(3): 177–188

Miller, R., Brown, H. & Mangan, C. (2016) *Integrated Care in Action: A Practical Guide for Health, Social Care and Housing Support*, London: Jessica Kingsley Publishers

Pratt, J., Plamping, D. & Gordon, P. (1999) *Partnership: Fit for Purpose?*, London: King's Fund

Priest, J. (2012) *The Integration of Health and Social Care*, London: British Medical Association

Royal College of Nursing (2017) *Integrating Health and Social Care across the UK: Toolkit for Nursing Leaders*, London: RCN

Shaw, S., Rosen, R. & Rumbold, B. (2011) *What Is Integrated Care?: An Overview of Integrated Care in the NHS*, London: Nuffield Trust

Vangen, S. & Huxham, C. (2012) The Tangled Web: Unravelling the Principle of Common Goals in Collaborations, *Journal of Public Administration Research & Theory*, 22(4): 731–760

Ward, V. (2017) *Knowledge Sharing across Health and Social Care Boundaries*, Leeds: University of Leeds

Watson, J. (2012) *Integrating Health and Social Care from an International Perspective*, London: International Longevity Centre UK

Wilson, S., Davison, N. & Casebourne, J. (2016) *Local Public Service Reform: Supporting Learning to Integrate Services and Improve Outcomes*, London: Institute for Government

Wilson, S., Davison, N., Clarke, M. & Casebourne, J. (2015) *Joining Up Public Services Around Local, Citizen Needs: Perennial Challenges and Insights on How to Tackle Them*, London: Institute for Government

Integrated care: England

Alderwick, H., Dunn, H., McKenna, H., Walsh, N. & Ham, C. (2016) *Sustainability and Transformation Plans in the NHS*, London: Kings Fund

Bate, A. (2017) *Health and Social Care Integration*, London: House of Commons Library

Beveridge, J., Burkett, M., Owens-Nash, G., Quick, H., Whittingham, A. & McDougall, A. (2017) *Health and Social Care Integration*, London: National Audit Office

Cameron, A., Lart, R., Bostock, L. & Coomber, C. (2012) *Factors that Promote and Hinder Joint and Integrated Working between Health and Social Care Services*, London: Social Care Institute for Excellence

Cheetham, M., Visram, S., Rushmer, R., Greig, G., Gibson, E., Khazaeli, B. & Wiseman, A. (2017) 'It Is Not a Quick Fix': Structural and Contextual Issues that Affect Implementation of Integrated Health and Well-Being Services: A Qualitative Study from North East England, *Public Health*, 152: 99–107

Creese, J. (2017) *Health and Social Care Integration: Confronting the Challenge*, Bristol: Eduserv

Department of Health (1998) *Partnership in Action*, London: Department of Health

Erens, B., Wistow, G., Durand, M., Mounier-Jack, S., Manacorda, T., Douglas, N., Hoomans, T. & Mays, N. (2017) *Evaluation of the Integrated Care and Support Pioneers Programme (2015–2020): Results from the First Survey (Spring 2016) of Pioneer Key Informants*, London: Policy Innovation Research Unit, London School of Hygiene & Tropical Medicine

Exworthy, M., Powell, M. & Glasby, J. (2017) The Governance of Integrated Health and Social Care in England: Great Expectations Not Met Once Again?, *Health Policy*, 121(11): 1124–1130

Fillingham, D., Jones, B. & Pereira, P. (2016) *The Challenge and Potential of Whole System Flow: Improving the Flow of People, Information and Resources across Whole Health and Social Care Economies*, London: The Health Foundation

Gilburt, H. (2016) *Supporting Integration through New Roles and Working across Boundaries*, London: Kings Fund

Groen, B. (2016) Why Integrated Healthcare Is Harder than We Think: How Social Cognitive Processes Hinder Successful Health and Care Service Delivery, *Journal of Enterprise Transformation*, 6(3–4): 120–135

Ham, C. (2018) *Making Sense of Integrated Care Systems, Integrated Care Partnerships and Accountable Care Organisations in the NHS in England*, London: Kings Fund

Ham, C. & Alderwick, H. (2015) *Place Based Systems of Care: A Way Forward for the NHS in England*, London: Kings Fund

Ham, C., Heenan, D., Longley, M. & Steel, D. (2013) *Integrated Care in Northern Ireland, Scotland and Wales: Lessons for England*, London: King's Fund

Health and Social Care Committee (2018) *Integrated Care: Organisations, Partnerships and Systems*, London: House of Commons

Holbourn, A. & Westwood, D. (2017) *Manchester: Local System Review Report: Health and Wellbeing Board*, London: Care Quality Commission

Holder, H. & Buckingham, H. (2017) *A Two-Way Street?: What Can CCGs Teach Us about Accountability in STPs?*, London: Nuffield Trust

Holder, H., Kumpunen, S., Castle-Clarke, S. & Lombardo, S. (2018) *Managing the Hospital and Social Care Interface: Interventions Targeting Older Adults*, London: Nuffield Trust

Howarth, J., Davis, D., Worsley-Cox, K., Brumby, J. & Fleming, R. (2017) Citizen-Led Healthcare: Learning from the Millom Experience, *International Journal of Integrated Care*, 17(5)

Humphries, R. (2015) Integrated Health and Social Care in England: Progress and Prospects, *Health Policy*, 119(7): 856–859

Johnstone, L., Rozansky, D., Dorrans, S., Dussin, L. & Barker, T. (2017) *Integration 2020: Scoping Research: Report to the Department Of Health*, London: Social Care Institute for Excellence

Laycock, K., Borrows, M. & Dobson, B. (2017) *Getting into Shape: Delivering a Workforce for Integrated Care*, London: Reform

Local Government Association (2016) *Efficiency Opportunities through Health and Social Care Integration: Delivering More Sustainable Health and Social Care*, London: Local Government Association

Local Government Association (2016) *Stepping Up to Place: Integration Self-Assessment Tool*, London: Local Government Association

Malby, B. & Anderson-Wallace, M. (2017) *Networks in Healthcare: Managing Complex Relationships*, Bingley: Emerald

NHS Confederation (2016) *Stepping Up to the Place: The Key to Successful Health and Social Care Integration*, London: Local Government Association/NHS Confederation/Association of Directors of Adult Social Services/NHS Clinical Commissioners

NHS England (2016) *People Helping People: Year Two of the Pioneer Programme*, London: NHS

NHS England (2015) *Integrated Care Pioneers: One Year On*, London: NHS

Pimperl, A. (2018) Re-Orienting the Model of Care: Towards Accountable Care Organisations, *International Journal of Integrated Care*, 18(1)

Richardson, B., Carnall, S., Gault, W. & Coleridge, A. (2016) *The Journey to Integration: Learning from Seven Leading Localities*, London: Carnall Farrar for Local Government Association

Richmond Group/New Philanthropy Capital (2018) *Tapping the Potential: Lessons from the Richmond Group's Practical Collaborative Work in Somerset*, London: The Richmond Group

Serlin, A., Whittingham, A. & Murphie, A. (2018) *The Health and Social Care Interface*, London: National Audit Office

Thorlby, R., Starling, A., Broadbent, C. & Watt, T. (2018) *What's the Problem with Social Care, and Why Do We Need to Do Better?*, London: Health Foundation/ Institute for Fiscal Studies/Kings Fund/Nuffield Trust

Integrated care: Scotland

Audit Scotland (2015) *Health and Social Care Integration*, Edinburgh: Audit Scotland

Audit Scotland (2018) *Health and Social Care Integration: Update On Progress*, Edinburgh: Audit ScotlandHendry, A. (2016) Creating an Enabling Political Environment for Health and Social Care Integration, *International Journal of Integrated Care*, 16(4)

Hendry, A., Taylor, A., Mercer, S. & Knight, P. (2016) Improving Outcomes through Transformational Health and Social Care Integration: The Scottish Experience, *Healthcare Quality*, 19(2): 73–79

Hutchison, K. (2015) An Exploration of the Integration of Health and Social Care within Scotland: Senior Stakeholders' Views of the Key Enablers and Barriers, *Journal of Integrated Care*, 23(3): 129–142

Miller, E., Whoriskey, M. & Cook, A. (2008) Outcomes for Users and Carers in the Context of Health and Social Care Partnership Working: From Research to Practice, *Journal of Integrated Care*, 16(2): 21–28

Petch, A. (2013) *Delivering Integrated Care and Support*, Glasgow: Association of Directors of Social Work/Institute for Research and Innovation in Social Services

Petch, A., Cook, A. & Miller, E. (2013) Partnership Working and Outcomes: Do Health and Social Care Partnerships Deliver for Users and Carers?, *Health & Social Care in the Community*, 21(6): 623–633

Scottish Government (2015) *Facilitating the Journey of Integration: A Guide for Those Supporting the Formation of Integration Joint Boards*, Edinburgh: Scottish Social Services Council/Social Work Scotland/NHS Education for Scotland/Scottish Government

Integrated care: Northern Ireland

Birrell, D. & Heenan, D. (2014) Integrated Care Partnerships in Northern Ireland: Added Value or Added Bureaucracy?, *Journal of Integrated Care*, 22(5–6): 197–207

Department of Health (2016) *Systems, Not Structures: Changing Health and Social Care: Expert Panel Report*, Belfast: Department of Health, Northern Ireland

Department of Health (2016) *Health and Wellbeing 2026: Delivering Together*, Belfast: Department of Health, Northern Ireland

Donaldson, L., Rutter, P. & Henderson, M. (2014) *The Right Time, the Right Place: An Expert Examination of the Application of Health and Social Care Governance Arrangements for Ensuring the Quality of Care Provision in Northern Ireland*, Belfast: Department of Health, Northern Ireland

Integrated care: Wales

Greenwell, S. (2017) A New Health and Social Care Context in Wales: Promoting Resilience through a Shift in Perspective and Different Relationships, *Journal of Integrated Care*, 25(4): 265–270

Thomas, M. & Llewellyn, M. (2018) *Working for a Shared Common Purpose: Experiences in Health and Social Care Integration in Wales*, Pontypridd: Welsh Institute for Health & Social Care, for UNISON

Welsh Assembly (2018) *A Revolution from Within: Transforming Health and Care in Wales: The Parliamentary Review of Health and Social Care in Wales: Final Report*: Cardiff: Welsh Assembly

Welsh Government (2018) *A Healthier Wales: Our Plan for Health and Social Care*, Cardiff: Welsh Government

Managing change

Abercrombie, R., Boswell, K. & Thomasoo, R. (2018) *Thinking Big: How to Use Theory of Change for Systems Change*, London: New Philanthropy Capital

Abercrombie, R., Harries, E. & Wharton, R. (2015) *Systems Change: A Guide to What It Is and How to Do It*, London: New Philanthropy Capital

Amoo, N., Malby, R. & Mervyn, K. (2016) Innovation and Sustainability in a Large-Scale Healthcare Improvement Collaborative: Seven Propositions for Achieving System-Wide Innovation and Sustainability, *International Journal of Sustainable Strategic Management*, 5(2): 149–179

Billiald, S. & McAllister-Jones, L. (2015) *Behaving Like a System?: The Preconditions for Place Based Systems Change*, London: Collaborate CIC/Lankelly Chase

Carter, A. & Varney, S. (2018) *Change Capability in the Agile Organisation*, Brighton: Institute for Employment Studies

Dougall, D., Lewis, M. & Ross, S. (2018) *Transformational Change in Health and Care: Reports from the Field*, London: Kings Fund

Edmonstone, J. (2010) A New Approach to Project Managing Change, *British Journal of Healthcare Management*, 16(5): 114–119

Fillingham, D. & Massey, L. (2018) *A Sense of Urgency, a Sense of Hope: A Culture and System for Continuous Improvement*, Sale: Advancing Quality Alliance

Leadbeater, C. (2013) *The Systems Innovator: Why Successful Innovation Goes Beyond Products*, London: NESTA

Mervyn, K. & Amoo, N. (2014) *Brief Literature Review on Improvement at Systems Level*, Leeds: Leeds Institute for Quality Healthcare

Mouser, A., Bowers, A. & Saltmarshe, E. (2017) *Systems Changers: "From Where I Stand": How Frontline Workers Can Contribute to and Create System Change: A Report on the 2016 System Changers Programme*, London: Lankelly Chase

Nabatu, H. & Evans, A. (2017) *Historical Review of Place Based Systems*, London: Lankelly Chase/Institute for Voluntary Action Research

Plamping, D., Gordon, P. & Pratt, J. (2010) *Supporting Change in Complex Adaptive Systems*, London: The Health Foundation

Plamping, D., Gordon, P. & Pratt, J. (2009) *Innovation and Public Services: Insights from Evolution*, Leeds: Centre for Innovation in Health Management, University of Leeds

Randle, A. (2016) *Systems Change in Public Services: A Discussion Paper*, London: Collaborate

Randle, A. & Anderson, H. (2016) *Building Collaborative Places: Infrastructure for System Change*, London: Lankelly Chase/Collaborate

Sustainable Improvement Team & Horizons Team (2018) *Leading Large Scale Change: A Practical Guide*, Leeds: NHS England

Systems leadership

Baylis, A. & Trimble, A. (2018) *Leading across Health and Social Care in Scotland: Learning from Chief Officers' Experience, Planning Next Steps*, London: Kings Fund

Benington, J. & Hartley, J. (2009) *'Whole Systems Go!': Improving Leadership across the Whole Public Service System: Propositions to Stimulate Discussion and Reform*, Sunningdale: National School of Government

Better Care Fund (2015) *How To … Lead and Manage Better Care Implementation*, London: Department of Health/Department for Communities and Local Government/Local Government Association/NHS England

BLC (2015) *Reframing, Realignment and Relationships: Interim Evaluation of the First Place-Based Programmes for Systems Leadership: Local Vision*, Bristol: University of the West of England

Bolden, R., Gulati, A., Ahmad, Y., Burgoyne, J., Chapman, N., Edwards, G., Green, E., Owen, D., Smith, I. & Spirit, M. (2015) *The Difference that Makes the Difference: Final Evaluation of the First Place-Based Programme for Systems Leadership: Local Vision*, Bristol: University of the West of England

Cairns, A., Cooper, A., Fox, A., Gilby, S.Hill, B., Malby, B., Straight, J., Walsh, J. & Wilderspin, J. (2015) *'Doing' Systems Leadership: Lessons from the Leadership Indaba*, Leeds: Centre for Innovation in Health Management, University of Leeds

Dalton, M., Jarvis, J., Powell, B. & Sorkin, D. (2015) *The Revolution Will Be Improvised: Part 2: Insights from Places on Transforming Systems*, The Leadership Centre

Department of Health (2015) *How to Lead and Manage Better Care Implementation*, London: Department of Health/Department of Communities and Local Government/Local Government Association/NHS England

Department of Health (2017) *HSC Collective Leadership Strategy*, Belfast: Department of Health, Northern Ireland

Edmonstone, J. (2017) *Action Learning in Health, Social and Community Care: Principles, Practices and Resources*, Abingdon: CRC Press

Evans, J., Daub, S., Goldhar, J., Wojtak, A. & Purbhoo, D. (2016) Leading Integrated Health and Social Care Systems: Perspectives from Research and Practice, *Healthcare Quarterly*, 18(4): 30–35

Fillingham, D. & Weir, B. (2014) *Systems Leadership: Lessons and Learning from AQuA's Integrated Care Discovery Communities*, London: Kings Fund

Ghate, D., Lewis, J. & Welbourn, D. (2013) *Systems Leadership: Exceptional Leadership for Exceptional Times: Synthesis Paper*, London: ADCS Virtual Staff College/The Leadership Forum/Colebrook Centre for Evidence & Implementation/Cass Business School, City University, London

Goss, S. (2015) *Systems Leadership: A View from the Bridge*, London: Office for Public Management

Heifetz, R. (1994) *Leadership without Easy Answers*, London: Belknap Press of Harvard University Press

Heifitz, R., Grashow, A. & Linsky, M. (2009) *The Practice of Adaptive Leadership: Tools and Tactics for Changing your Organisation and the World*, Boston: Harvard Business Publishing

Hulke, S., Walsh, N., Powell, M., Ham, C. & Alderwick, H. (2017) *Leading across the Health and Care System: Lessons from Experience*, London: Kings Fund

Hunter, D. (2017) The Systems Leadership Challenge Facing the Primary Care Workforce, *European Journal of Public Health*, 27(3)

Kelley-Patterson, D. (2012) What Kind of Leadership Does Integrated Care Need?, *London Journal of Primary Care*, 5(1): 3–7

Klinga, C., Hansson, J., Hasson, H. & Sachs, M. (2016) Co-Leadership: A Management Solution for Integrated Health and Social Care, *International Journal for Integrated Care*, 16(2)

Levesque, J.-F., Harris, M., Scott, C., Crabtree, B., Miller, W., Halma, L., Hogg, W., Weenink, J.-W., Advocat, J., Gunn, J. & Russell, G. (2018) Dimensions and Intensity of Inter-Professional Teamwork in Primary Care: Evidence from Five International Jurisdictions, *Family Practice*, 35(3): 285–294

Lewis, M. (2016) *Adaptive Leadership: Embracing Chaos and Courage for Sustainable Change*, Cardiff: Academi Wales

McKimm, J. & Phillips, K. (2009) *Leadership and Management in Integrated Services*, Exeter: Learning Matters

MacDonald, I., Burke, C. & Stewart, K. (2006) *Systems Leadership: Creating Positive Organisations*, Abingdon: Routledge

Memon, A. & Kinder, T. (2015) Management in an Increasingly Collaborative and Integrated Public Sector: The Changing Managerial Role in the Scottish National Health Service and the Implications for Managerial Learning and Development, *International Journal of Public Administration*, 39(4): 1–14

Middleton, J. (2007) *Beyond Authority: Leadership in a Changing World*, Basingstoke: Palgrave Macmillan

Miller, R. (2018) *Developing Integrated Care: The Role of the Multidisciplinary Team*, London: Social Care Institute for Excellence

Miller, R., Combes, G., Brown, H. & Harwood, A. (2014) Inter-Professional Workplace Learning: A Catalyst for Strategic Change?, *Journal of Inter-Professional Care*, 28(3): 186–193

National Skills Academy for Social Care (2013) *Leadership Starts with Me: The Why, What and How of Leadership in Adult Social Care*, London: National Skills Academy

Needham, C. & Mangan, C. (2014) *The 21st Century Public Servant*, Birmingham: University of Birmingham for Economic & Social Research Council/Public Service Academy

NHS Improvement (2017) *Developing People – Improving Care: A National Framework for Action on Improvement and Leadership Development in NHS-Funded Services*, London: NHS

NHS Improvement (2017) Culture and Leadership Toolkit – https://improvement.nhs.uk/resources/culture-and-leadership/

NHS Leadership Academy (2016) *Developing Systems Leadership: Interventions, Options and Opportunities*, Leeds: NHS Leadership Academy

Obolensky, N. (2014) *Complex Adaptive Leadership: Embracing Paradox and Uncertainty* (2nd edition), Farnham: Gower Publishing

Scott, P., Harris, J. & Florek, A. (2016) *Systems Leadership for Effective Services: Occasional Report No. 2*, Nottingham: Local Government Association/Association of Directors of Children's Services/SOLACE/Virtual Staff College

Senge, P.Hamilton, H. & Kania, J. (2015) The Dawn of System Leadership, *Stanford Social Innovation Review*, Winter: 27–33

Sharp, C. (2018) *Learning and Outcomes from Leadership for Integration: Final Report*, Edinburgh: Research for Real for NHS Education for Scotland/Scottish Social Services Council/ Royal College of General Practitioners (Scotland)

Skills for Care (2017) *New Visions for Leadership: Supporting the Development of Leaders and Managers in Social Care*, Leeds: Skills for Care

Smith, T., Fowler-Davis, S., Nancarrow, S., Ariss, S. & Enderby, P. (Forthcoming) Leadership in Interprofessional Health and Social Care Teams: A Literature Review, *Leadership in Health Services*

Soutar, F., Warrander, J. & Henderson, J. (2017) *Exploring Collaborative Learning, Research and Action in Public Service Reform: Aberdeenshire Health and Social Care Change Fund beyond Action Learning Initiative*, Glasgow: What Works Scotland

Stacey, R. (2012) *Tools and Techniques of Leadership and Management: Meeting the Challenge of Complexity*, Abingdon: Routledge

Tate, W. (2009) *The Search for Leadership: An Organisational Perspective*, Charmouth: Triarchy Press

Timmins, N. (2015) *The Practice of Systems Leadership: Being Comfortable with Chaos*, London: Kings Fund

Vize, R. (2015) *Swimming Together or Sinking Alone: Health, Care and the Art of Systems Leadership*, London: Institute of Healthcare Management

Welbourn, D., Warwick, R., Carnall, C. & Fathers, D. (2012) *Leadership of Whole Systems*, London: Kings Fund

West, M., Eckert, R., Collins, B. & Chowla, R. (2017) *Caring to Change: How Compassionate Leadership Can Stimulate Innovation in Health Care*, London: Kings Fund

West, M., Eckhart, R., Stewart, K. & Pasmore, B. (2012) *Developing Collective Leadership for Healthcare*, London: Kings Fund

Worrall, R. & Leech, D. (2018) Will Place-Based Leadership Be the Right Remedy for Health and Social Care?, *British Journal of Healthcare Management*, 24(2): 90–94

INDEX

Note: page numbers in italic type refer to Figures; those in bold type refer to Tables.

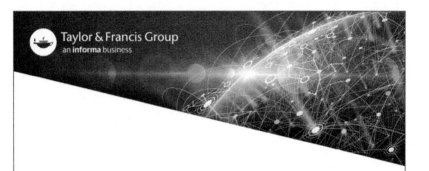